Angela Neustatter is a freelance writer. Her previous books include *Getting the Right Job*, *Working for Yourself* (with Chris Parsons) and *Parenthood, Warts and All* (with Caroline Foley). Gina Newson is a film-maker, who made *Mixed Feelings*, the film on which the book is based.

Mixed Feelings

The Experience of Abortion

Angela Neustatter

with Gina Newson

Pluto  **Press**

London   Sydney   Dover New Hampshire

First published in 1986 by Pluto Press Limited,
The Works, 105a Torriano Avenue, London NW5 2RX
and Pluto Press Australia Limited, PO Box 199, Leichhardt,
New South Wales 2040, Australia. Also Pluto Press,
51 Washington Street, Dover, New Hampshire 03820 USA

7   6   5   4   3   2   1

90   89   88   87   86

Set by Rapidset and Design Ltd, London WC1.
Printed in Great Britain by Guernsey Press Co. Ltd.
Guernsey, C.I.

British Library Cataloguing in Publication Data
Neustatter, Angela
  Mixed feelings : the experience of
  abortion.
  1.   Abortion
  I.   Title   II.   Newson, Gina
  363.4'6'0922   HQ767

ISBN 07453 0027 8

Contents

Acknowledgements

Thanks first and foremost to all the women and men who shared their feelings with us, providing unique and valuable insights.

Enormous gratitude to Caroline Bailey who went through drafts of this book and made invaluable suggestions and comments.

Thanks, too, to Joanna Chambers at the Birth Control Trust for providing research and contacts. Thanks to Romy Goodschild and Charlotte Owens at the Family Planning Association for opening their files to me, and thanks to Dr John Ashton at Liverpool University for enlightening discussion and for copies of the substantial amount of work he has done on the subject of abortion.

Jenny Levin and Alison Scott deserve thanks for the intelligent and thorough research they have done for this book; it was also good to exchange ideas with Gillian Clarke who was preparing a dissertation on counselling.

There is appreciation, too, for Pete Ayrton for his careful editing.

Angela Neustatter

My thanks to the women who appeared in the film *Mixed Feelings*: Mary Mortimer and her family, Pia Goddard, Susan Pearson, Sue Hunter, Maureen O'Connor, Caroline Stark, Sylvia Welczdo, Anna Raeburn as well as those who contributed with their many letters who had to remain anonymous and who, in sharing their experiences, provided the genesis of this book.

My thanks, too, to therapists Helen Davis and Clair

Chapman who took part in the film.

I would also like to thank producer Julian Aston who asked me to make the programme; researchers Sarah Aspinal and Roz Schwartz; Commissioning Editor for Channel Four TV, Carol Haslam, who was strongly supportive throughout and to Liz Rowland and all at Broadcasting Support Services, who with Channel Four helped women to form self-help groups across the country after the programme was transmitted.

Gina Newson

Mixed Feelings

Introduction

In 1982 Gina Newson made the film *Mixed Feelings*, which focused on the human rather than the campaigning experience of abortion. In the film women came together to talk about the feelings they had in going through an abortion, the ambivalence, conflict and isolation many experienced, as well as some more positive feelings.

The film touched a nerve. After the programme ended more than 1,000 women phoned in to the Broadcasting Support Services to ask for information about setting up abortion self-help groups, to express their relief at seeing that other women felt as they did. Yet more wrote letters saying the same thing.

It all showed very clearly the need there is to open up abortion as a subject which can be talked about. For although the politics are constantly in the news , publicly discussed, the individual women who go through an abortion so often feel they cannot speak out about it. The taboo on the personal feelings around this issue is very strong.

And so a book which would follow on from the film's important beginning, seemed a good idea. It was suggested by Pete Ayrton, the editor, who admired *Mixed Feelings* and approached Gina Newson. She suggested that I should write it, partly because I am a journalist concerned with women's issues, but equally importantly because I had taken part in the film, speaking about my own feelings when I had an abortion.

Although I have always marched and campaigned for a woman's right to choose, along with so many of my contemporaries, when it came to deciding to end a pregnancy, I was shocked by the distress and confusion I felt. I did not like having to take personal responsibility for ending a life, even though I believe that women have to make this choice when the odds make a child seem intolerable. My partner and I with two young children, uncertain jobs and financial difficulties felt that another child would have put unbearable pressures onto life. For all that, I felt intensely sad that it was not possible to welcome another child into our life and I did not much like myself for what I was choosing to do.

For several months afterwards I experienced a curious upheaval of the emotions; an unaccustomed sense of nihilism; a turbulence in my private life which I felt unable to control. The feelings subsided and passed. I still regret not having been able to have the third child. I still think about it, but I am sure it was not the wrong decision, just a sad one.

I am telling this because I believe that in writing a book like this it is essential to understand the nature of the dilemma and because my own mixed feelings around the event have set my perspective for this book which is intended to take a crack at the taboo, to open up some of the emotion, guilt, pain, silence women have when they choose termination, as well as pointing to the resourcefulness many show in coping.

I have drawn together material from 150 women and 25 men, and although it is not intended as a scientific survey, I have included a good deal of research as well as interviews with experts, and statistics, to support my own findings. But the basis of the book is the words of those who have talked about their abortions.

To contact the people who have contributed, I placed letters in newspapers and magazines around the country with the aim of getting a class and geographical cross-section. Gina Newson, when preparing her film, put a letter in *Woman* magazine which drew a large response, and the ideas, feelings and experiences described by these writers have been used to add to the picture of what abortion means in human terms.

The book is written chronologically: finding out that you are pregnant and the impact this has, through to making the decision to have an abortion, arranging it, having the operation and feelings after the abortion. The book ends with an access chapter giving information about how and where to go for help if you have an unplanned pregnancy, and the kind of support which is available.

An obvious omission in the book is the issue of abortion when an ante-natal test shows that the child is handicapped. I have quoted one case where a woman suspects the child could be handicapped and chooses abortion, but I have not made it a central theme because I believe this is a separate issue with particular morals and dilemmas involved which require a book to themselves.

No doubt this book will be labelled 'pro-abortion' by those who oppose abortion because it presents the arguments why a great many people (myself included) believe that the women who will bear children of unplanned pregnancies must, ultimately, be the ones to decide whether they will do this. But it is not intended as a campaigning book. It contains case histories where women feel regret and immense sadness at having chosen abortion, it contains words from women who are not certain whether they have made the right choice.

Because the politics of abortion are so heated – the lobby which supports woman's choice and the anti-abortionists so fiercely polarized – discussion of feelings about the experience of abortion tend to be used to propagandize and make points. Thus the pro-choice lobby will present women who have gone through their terminations without any adverse feelings and who have emerged strengthened from the experience, while the anti-abortionists will produce saddened, depressed women who feel they are traumatized for life by what they have done.

Yet if these extremes exist they are not the stuff of my interviews. The women who have self-selected themselves for this book have revealed more complex emotions; they have described pain turning to strength, resilience breaking down into despair; distress and acceptance, stoicism and sadness mixed. They have told the human dimension to abortion.

Angela Neustatter

1. Thinking About Abortion

When I found out I was pregnant I felt good, right, excited. It was a crazy feeling really because my life at the time was absolutely not set up to have a child. I couldn't have coped financially or practically without huge difficulty. But still a primitive, unthinking bit of me was delighted to find that I actually functioned like a woman, that my body could create a baby. (Jane)

I didn't want a child. I had never wanted one and our marriage had been happy and contented without. Then I got pregnant because of contraceptive failure and although I knew I did not want a child, that this situation was in every sense a mistake, I did feel a strange pleasure in the idea that if I did nothing a child could develop. But that didn't seem reason to give birth to a child who was not wanted. (Myra)

I was eighteen when I got pregnant by my boyfriend. I thought it was love and I was delighted as I liked the idea of us all together with a baby. But he kept saying, 'Don't do it – it'll spoil your life,' and what he meant of course was that it would spoil his life. I didn't feel I could do it alone – I've seen too many trying and it's not good. (Lesley)

Girls learn at a very young age that they will grow up to become mothers. It is a conviction, a dominant theme to the female existence in our culture. It begins when the little girl receives her first baby doll, a cuddly copy of the children she is assumed to want from that time on; and it continues when parents deliver their anxious talk on the facts of life. The first romance is more often than not built on a fantasy

of that most conventional perfect bliss which Irma Kurtz
describes as 'mum, dad and two beautiful kids in a rose-
covered cottage', while the marriage ceremony, in which
most participate, is generally seen as a woman's declaration
of her readiness to become wife and mother, childbearer
and child carer.

Biological destiny is the name of the game and it takes a
peculiar kind of conviction to say you don't want to play
when its rewards are mirrored everywhere. The persuasive,
pervasive images of women as mothers infiltrate our lives
from the simpering 'perfect' mums whose crises revolve
around stains on a soccer shirt or children spurning the
selected breakfast cereal, to the glamorized stars of the big
screen who so often appear to be able to incorporate the
rigours of motherhood into the life they led before.
Women's magazines provide a fascinating and confusing
double bind by carrying, on the one hand, thoughtful, serious articles on the very real conflicts many women experience in the role of mother, and then defusing the impact by
surrounding the article with reassuring shots of mothers
cuddling babies or playing with divine toddlers.

Implicit in the sentimentalized picture of mothering
which is beamed out to us all, all the time, is not just that
bringing up children is the ultimate fulfilment, but also that
it is justification for an existence. There is no act, no piece of
productivity, which will bring society's affection and
approval in the way having a baby does. As Linda Gordon,[1]
examining the practical and psychic control society operates over woman's fertility, says: 'Girls are socialized from
their own infancies to anticipate motherhood. Women
learn to like themselves in mothering roles, which allow
them experiences of love and power not easily found in
other situations.' Given that, for many women, such satisfactions from life as a pleasing career, earning a good
income of her own, a satisfying relationship and a stimulat-
ing environment are not available, it is understandable that

having children is a way of validating life and achieving a feeling of importance.

The impulse to have children, to fulfil a deeply conditioned instinct and to gain the public seal of approval is understandably very strong. While there is no doubt that for a great many women having children is a deeply rewarding process, it also requires a dedication and commitment which may well conflict with a woman's other, deeply felt aspirations and desires and may well introduce unexpected pressures and deprivations into her life. Yet this reality is rarely balanced against the publicized satisfactions and pleasures of mothering.

Feminism, with its challenge to the prime valuation of women as childbearers, has gone some way towards examining what mothering means for a woman. The conflicts of child-rearing, the difficulties of being a single mother, of bringing up children in poverty, of coping with the tug between a woman's needs and her child's, have been brought out into the open. Women have met together and in the 'safety' of supportive groups or among friends, have talked about the difficulties, the disillusionment, the sense of being consumed by the needs of a child, the loss of personal status and perhaps a career, the lack of 'maternal instinct'.

The women's movement has allowed women to admit that mothering is not always their final goal, that a culturally defined role may not necessarily be right for them. And as the sentimental mythology has been questioned, so women – particularly younger women – have begun to see that education, a career, personal freedom and independence are legitimate aspirations. It is this thinking, this belief that a woman may choose her own needs over inevitable childbearing, which has inspired the forceful movement which supports the right to choose abortion.

This opening up of the subject has certainly allowed women to talk more freely and honestly about what mothering actually entails, to kick hard the notion that the female sex is innately programmed to motherhood and that therefore this 'natural' process is effortless. Yet for most women, the conviction remains that they will at some time fulfil cultural expectations by becoming pregnant and giving birth.

Having children is the most perfect demonstration of femaleness and a reassurance to a patriarchal society that women, who take most of the responsibility in child-rearing, will continue to slot into their place. A lot is invested in women as mothers. On the one hand, they have thus far been prepared to do many years of hard work in bringing up a new generation, often for remarkably little reward or thanks and, on the other, they are conveniently kept out of the labour market or at least prevented from competing for the best-paid and most prestigious jobs by the demands of bringing up a family.

Looked at from this perspective it is not surprising that those women who do not have babies face society's disapproval, and never more so than when, having conceived, they resort to abortion. So strong is the feeling that woman's role is as mother, that disapproval extends to even those women who cannot have children. Throughout history, the barren woman has been stigmatized, while infertility has been and still is threatened as punishment for the woman who is promiscuous or aborts her child.

Fertility is demonstrable womanliness which reassures society that the status quo is not seriously threatened, that women are continuing to desire and conform to their 'natural' role. As Marion Hall and Raymond Illsley note,[2] implicit in not wanting children and legitimizing abortion as a way of preventing children, is a profound threat to established social institutions: 'Family, marriage and parenthood are such fundamental institutions in all societies that they are surrounded with strong sanctions. The intention of such sanctions is to induce individuals to accept as moral and desirable, a particular pattern of behaviour, to deter them from contravening moral rules.'

It is clear then, that the pressures for women to want children and to have the children they conceive are powerful. When a woman becomes pregnant, however disastrous it might logically appear to be in the context of her life, there is a powerful impulse to believe that being pregnant *is* the right thing, that a child should be born. This feeling may well be in fierce conflict with the reality of the situation in which the woman finds herself; it may be in opposition to a certainty that she does *not* want children; it may profoundly threaten a treasured vocation or aspiration, but the impulse to believe that the unplanned pregnancy is more important than the practical considerations is immensely strong. And so it is that many women who go on to choose abortion and who believe that it is the only possible and appropriate solution for them, nevertheless experience painful and confusing feelings. Barbara voices her feelings:

> I became pregnant with a coil in place. As we were using contraception, my partner and I had chosen not to have children – it was not part of our relationship. Yet there it was, against all odds growing inside me. The pregnancy filled my mind. I read bits I could find. I bought a picture book of the growing foetus and noticed all kinds of signs in my body. My body had achieved something. It was forcing me to look at something I had avoided. I felt then I knew I did want to have children in my life, and actually making one seemed very special.
>
> Alongside this feeling was despair about what would happen to *me*. I could leave my job, but what would replace it? I don't have a rosy-eyed view of motherhood. I felt I knew how much hard work it would be and that it would not satisfy many of my needs. I could feel the shadow of future resentment and the anger I would feel towards the child. I couldn't see how in the time I had, I could arrange things so that I could be a good and

healthy parent. My partner didn't want it and although I know lots of women do manage alone, I wanted to choose not to.

Ellen, 28, speaks for a number of women interviewed in wishing the circumstances had permitted her to have the child and bring it up in the way she wished, but she felt that the risk to the child's future happiness and well-being was great in the circumstances and so she chose abortion.

I became pregnant soon after taking on a mortgage on my flat where I lived alone. I had split up a while back with a man I loved very much, and I suppose I was looking for that closeness and caring again. I did meet a man who I cared for very much, quite quickly, and we began to sleep together. He made no secret of his wish to be free, not to have commitments or ties, so when I found I was pregnant, I knew deep down that it was a sad situation, although I tried hard to pretend otherwise.

When I told him, as I suspected, he immediately suggested an abortion. I was angry and so hurt with him for that, although it was really only what he had always let me know.

But I felt angry and resentful that a time which I had always believed would be so joyful was, instead, painful and disgusting. I felt cheated and that I'd been robbed of that beautiful first (wanted) pregnancy feeling you hear of. It was just the wrong time to find out that I could conceive.

Sadness at not being able to celebrate pregnancy, to enjoy the sense of specialness it brings, is an understandable response. At the same time, abortion is a situation in which women take control of their lives and make decisions about when and under what circumstances they will become childbearers. The decision may be an unhappy one, full of regrets, but nevertheless it is one which the woman is in certain circumstances legally permitted, and in the eyes of a great many people, morally entitled, to make. Since 1967, a great many women have been making the decision publicly and visibly.

Although, in their role as policy-makers, doctors and also partners, many men do oppose a woman's right to choose, it would be wrong to suggest that the opposition for abortion is male-dominated. In fact, leading the anti-abortion campaign are women like Nuala Scarisbrik, organizer of LIFE and Phyllis Bowman, Chairwoman of the Society for the Protection of the Unborn Child (SPUC) and Debby Sanders, founder member of Women for Life, which describes itself as a feminist anti-abortion group, while many of the rank and file supporters of these groups are women. These women are active with particular zeal, fired by the fact that abortion seems an unacceptable choice to those who have built their lives around the importance of procreation, who have sacrificed their own ambitions and aspirations. In her book, *The Politics of Motherhood*,[3] Kristin Lukas discusses how a high proportion of women active in the anti-abortion lobby in America have made family life and bringing up children absolutely primary in their lives; have dedicatedly turned their backs on the demanding and traditionally 'male' idea of commitment to work and dedication to personal success. Lukas writes:

> Women who oppose abortion and seek to make it officially unavailable are declaring both practically and symbolically that women's reproductive roles should be given social primacy . . . It is obvious that this view is supportive of women who have already decided that their familial and reproductive roles are the major ones in their lives.
>
> So, quite aside from any religious or moral determination that any conception has the right to grow to term and be born, abortion is an acknowledgement

that pregnancy is not biological destiny, that a woman
has not only failed to control her fertility in the approved
way, but that she is also preparing to reject the
consequences of this.

There is a tendency for anti-abortionists to see those who
support the right to abortion as having at best a callous
indifference to the implications of termination and at worst
some kind of rapacious pleasure in seeing women exercising 'choice' and choosing abortion. In fact, for many
feminists in the pro-choice lobby, abortion is a lesser of two
evils; a sad and regrettable choice but one they see women
making – and making too when abortion is illegal and
involves terrible risk – because there seems no other way.
For example, the writer and theologian Sara Maitland
rejects abortion as a personal choice but expresses this
view: 'I feel that the world has become so subverted, per-
verted in its entirety, that the perversion of abortion is a
structural necessity. It's the only thing that we can do sometimes' – and she follows this with an impassioned plea for
action to make a 'society in which abortion is a much less
attractive option'.[4]

Nor are pro-abortion women free from personal conflict.
Kathleen McDonnell describes the unexpected, ambivalent feelings she had after the birth of her daughter. 'There is
a realization emerging that abortion hits us at the very core
of our female socialization. With abortion, as with other
areas of our reproductive lives, women are at a historical
juncture, finding ourselves faced with new and unpre-
cedented choices, choices for which history and our condi-
tioning have ill prepared us.'[5]

2. Pregnancy: Finding Out

I'd had a relationship with a man who went abroad and I'd been on my own feeling very low, for a while. Then, quite unexpectedly, he returned and came to see me. I actually didn't think that we would sleep together, but it happened and I wasn't prepared. I suppose I thought I'd get away with it. But then I missed a period and I started feeling really nauseous and wretched and I knew. Of course I knew. I was a grown woman, not a child and I was horrified. I remember doing a home pregnancy kit and seeing the brown ring and my stomach just turned over. I couldn't kid myself it wasn't true any longer. (Pat)

I got pregnant because of a contraceptive failure so there was no question of us having considered the possibility or of us wanting a child. I already had one and my boyfriend, who has a very low opinion of himself, always said he didn't want children. So when I got the result of my pregnancy test and it was positive I felt panic-stricken. My boyfriend went into a deep depression and I was very aware from that first moment of knowing that this was my problem; I would have to get on and solve it. (Valerie)

My husband was due to have a vasectomy when I got pregnant. He had decided on that because the youngest of our three children has a hereditary handicap which makes him very demanding and hard work. There was a real risk that another boy would have the same problem and we both felt that was a risk we couldn't take. Already I felt my daughters got too little time and attention. So when I found I was pregnant I was devastated. It was the worst moment I can remember in my life. I so desperately didn't want to be pregnant, I didn't want to have to face the situation. I have never believed in abortion and I hate the idea that, as a society, we cannot cope with handicapped people. And yet looking at our life – we have very little money, a tiny house and, as I said, I am stretched as it is with the little boy and his sisters to cope with – I could see what a situation it would create. It wasn't just whether I could cope with one handicapped child, but possibly with two. And then there was the effect it would have on the others. I just broke down and cried when the doctor told me I was expecting. I just sobbed and sobbed and he was that kind but of course he couldn't sort it out. (Janet)

Each year some 140,000 women decide that their unplanned pregnancies cannot go on. For these women, confirmation means confronting a reality most of us do not consider until there is no alternative. It is this moment which strips away any possibility that the all-too-identifiable symptoms just might be flu, a phantom pregnancy, nerves, stress or any of the other explanations women offer themselves when they don't want pregnancy to be the truth.

Kay left school, illiterate, at the age of 15 and spent the next 15 years scratching together a living in a number of 'not very desirable' ways. At the age of 30 she employed a private tutor, learned to read and write and started a student organization for other illiterate adults. She was 36, with her own small shop in the centre of London, and married when she became pregnant.

I knew within days of conceiving that I was pregnant. I had every classic symptom – I felt sick, and so nauseous during the day that I couldn't work. I'd always wanted children but my husband didn't so I didn't feel jubilant or pleased, only very upset.

June, who lives and works in a small rural town, was 19

when she 'fell pregnant' by the boy, one and a half years younger, that she was seeing.

I was madly in love and having never had a sexual relationship before, I didn't realize how quickly one can become pregnant. I don't know who was more shattered when my test was confirmed, my boyfriend or me. Immediately I knew I didn't want that baby even though he did. I just felt it was a trap, it would make my life impossible.

For Myra, a 23-year-old working in the health service, the signs of pregnancy could not easily be ignored:

When I began to get swollen breasts and to feel tired I had a horrible suspicion deep down. But I was able to talk myself out of worrying until I missed a period. Then I did get really worried. I went to my GP and he sent off the test. So then I had to wait a few days. I could have done a home test, of course, but I chose not to – still trying to convince myself what I suspected wasn't real, I suppose.
  Then the results came through. I remember my GP telling me to sit down in this strange voice and that was when I knew, when there was no ducking what had happened. And it was horrible because I knew it couldn't be good news; that wasn't going to be possible with my life.

Nancy is married with two sons, the youngest has a hole in the heart and she describes with vivid recollection the strain it put on their relationship when he was little. It was at the time when the child was improving, when her marriage which had been through a 'very low' period was beginning to get better as she and her husband George were getting more time together, that Nancy became pregnant.

I knew immediately I was pregnant and my first reaction

was terror, absolute terror and horror because I think one of the reasons I got pregnant was that we were relaxing and enjoying ourselves at last. It was like a sort of punishment and very unfair as I had been using a cap. I felt I just couldn't take it, that emotionally I was not up to coping with being pregnant.

It is not surprising that many women speak of this moment, of finding out, with vivid recollection. For this is the time of reckoning, when the chance that the symptoms might be something else – a 'warning' to be more careful in future, just 'something I had brought on by worrying' – is stripped away. It is at this moment that the experience of abortion begins for those who go on to terminate.

The Lane Commission, when it surveyed the working of the Abortion Act, found that 'the vast majority who commented on this [personal reaction to pregnancy] felt horror, shock, fear'.

At the same time, women are caught by the ambivalence of their feelings. Sue voices this ambivalence:

I knew when I suspected pregnancy that I could not have a child. I have only a rented home, I have to work to earn and that's only just about enough to support myself. The man involved was not around so it seemed to me there was no way being pregnant could be a good thing. Yet I felt a curious, disturbing sense of being thrilled.

That was awful really because I couldn't allow myself to go with the feeling. I had to cut it off fast and try to be distanced about what was happening.

From a different perspective 39-year-old Valerie's feelings were similar:

I have three children and I felt sure I didn't want more, but when I got pregnant something inside me was making me feel good about it. I think it was memory of the fact that whenever I was pregnant before it had been the right thing, we'd been thrilled.

But this time John, my husband, was quite sure he didn't want another child and in honesty I felt the same. We were very hard up when the children were little; I was at home all the time and now that the youngest is ten we were beginning to lead lives for ourselves a bit. It really did seem to me that this pregnancy was a choice between me or the baby.

Not surprisingly the way a woman is treated when she first discovers an unplanned pregnancy is also poignantly remembered – the sensitivity or insensitivity of those dealing with her are keenly felt. Janet wrote:

The nurse came into the waiting room where I was sitting with all these other girls and she just said to me, 'It's positive' – like that, very unemotional and for me it was devastating. How could she be like that about something which was so shocking, so awful for me?

Lesley's doctor called her into his room:

He told me to sit down, very nicely, very gently and he asked me, 'How do you feel about having a baby?' and of course I knew then that the test was positive, but I felt he was giving me the chance to think about it. He wasn't telling me something and forcing me to react pleased or to say it's terrible.

I chatted with him a long while about why I thought I couldn't manage a kid, but that I hadn't thought about it properly because I hadn't known for sure the result. He then asked about my parents, about how I was living, my boyfriend. I think trying to help me see how it might be possible to have the child.

There are plenty of myths and superstitions in our society about who becomes pregnant by mistake and it is the very young, the lower classes and ethnic groups who are seen as having abortions. In fact, women from across the social and economic scale, from all ethnic groups and from all kinds of religious beliefs get pregnant in circumstances which lead them to choose termination.

Unplanned pregnancy occurs much more often among married women than among the unmarried, although twice as many abortions are performed on the unmarried, according to Professor François Lafitte, Director of the British Pregnancy Advisory Service (BPAS), who looked into abortion trends for the years 1973–81. This is not, of course, surprising when you consider that a child can generally be accommodated with considerably less problem into a two-parent, established family, where there may already be children, than into the life of a single woman who may well face financial hardship, isolation and censure, or a woman in a partnership which has not yet settled into a stable and permanent pattern.

The largest number of abortions is performed on the 25–34 age group, with the 16–24-year-olds making the next largest group. These figures, demonstrating clearly that it is the young and unmarried who have the most abortions, lead to the kind of thinking much favoured by our tabloid press, that our young are promiscuous and irresponsible and reflect clearly the evils of a permissive society. It is a view which Dr John Ashton, Senior Lecturer in Community Medicine at Liverpool University, who has done considerable work on teenage sexuality, questions:

> These statistics are often used to make a point about the immorality of the young, yet they tell us absolutely nothing about the number of partners young people tend to have, how often they have sex, how lightly or seriously they take it. In other words, they tell us nothing about moral attitudes or about how responsible the young are actually being.

Yet all sorts of conclusions are drawn and there is a popular image of the young as promiscuous and sexually irresponsible which in all the years I have spent working in this field I have not found to be a truthful, broad-based picture.

This is a point made, too, by Caroline Bailey at Brook Clinics, who draws the conclusion from her work that

the young tend to be very serious about their sex lives and are very likely to be mongamous. In fact we often find that girls who split up with their boyfriends then decide they must stop using contraception because they don't want to sleep with anyone else. The problem here is that they then have a passionate reunion, have not got contraception, and get pregnant.

One of the reasons that the teenage abortion rate is high is that the young no longer feel that having the child and getting married in order to legitimize it is the only option. Sue was 17 when she became pregnant by a long-standing boyfriend:

I did think about having the child, and so did he, but then we looked at what it would mean – he or I would have had to give up studying, the other would probably have had to try to get a job, any job, in order to support the family and that would have been the end of all our ambitions, all the things we have worked towards throughout our school years, all the hopes we have of offering kids when and if we do have them, a decent standard of living. So we chose abortion.

Wendy was 19 when she conceived in a relationship which had been 'going downhill' for a while. She says:

We weren't getting along well and I suppose the reason we were still sleeping together was the wish not to face up to parting; we were trying to convince ourselves it was still all right. Then I found I was pregnant and he actually said we could have it, he would marry me, but I just knew that wouldn't solve any of our problems. I just thought, imagine me stuck at home with a child, an unhappy marriage and probably eventually divorce. It just didn't seem the right thing to do. I didn't like the idea of abortion, it does seem like murder to me, but even so, it was preferable to destroying two grown peoples' lives.

The voices which come through the interviews for this book show clearly that the changing perspectives, the concern with women's rights throughout the past years, have had an impact on the thinking of the young of all classes. There is a clear recognition even by women who feel very bad about their abortions, who dislike themselves for doing it, that they were entitled to opt for continuing with education, a career, with a job which enables them to earn their own money, or with a relationship which is being explored and enjoyed in freedom, rather than having an unwanted child. It is a trend which Dr Judith Bury, researching patterns of teenage pregnancy, has understood as part of a wider scale of changing values.[6] She points out that in 1970 nearly half of teenagers who became pregnant when single married during the pregnancy, but that this proportion fell steadily so that by 1980 less than a quarter of unmarried teenagers legitimized the pregnancy in this way. She says: 'There has been a change in the attitude of teenagers towards an unintended pregnancy. Before the late 1960s when a teenager became pregnant, she often accepted this in a more or less fatalistic manner as an inevitable result of sexual activity, as there were few opportunities to prevent pregnancy for those who were sexually active and abortions were difficult to obtain.'

But while getting a termination may represent a better choice than proceeding with an unwanted pregnancy, with all that this entails, it is still an unhappy, unpleasant choice.

This needs saying to counteract the insidious suggestions which claim that when abortion is legal and available women use it as a form of contraception. It is a particuarly insulting suggestion when you listen to the distress and grief many women voice at feeling they must choose abortion. And even women who do not experience these intense emotions, who feel they have made a correct and reasonable choice, are quite clear that it has not been a pleasant thing to do and that they would not wish to have to make the choice again.

Why, at a time when contraceptives are easily and freely available, do so many unwanted pregnancies occur? One answer is that contraceptives are not satisfactory. Many women we interviewed for this book spoke of the problems they had in finding a satisfactory form of contraception. These included pain and bleeding with the IUD, unpleasant side-effects from the Pill; the messiness (as well as the higher risk) of the cap. Yet it is women who are expected to cope with this side of a sex life and who are blamed then expected to 'cope' with the problem if things go wrong.

Myrna, a mature student who had become pregnant trying the Billings natural birth control method, says:

> I knew that there was a risk I would get pregnant this way but the risk seemed better than pumping my body full of hormones for years. The Pill is a male-designed form of birth control and because they are not having to take it, to risk their health, they think we should take it and not get pregnant.
>
> I hated having an abortion and now I am trying with the cap again – although I find it quite inhibiting – but I do think it wrong that nothing satisfactory has been designed yet.

Gemma found she could use a coil for about three years, then 'my body would start protesting'. She explains: 'I found with both my coils that after this amount of time I got pains, abdominal aches and quite a lot of discomfort while having sex. I just felt my body was saying "enough" and I had to have them out. Then I tried a cap and my boyfriend used sheaths but we were unlucky because one broke and I got pregnant.' Although statistics demonstrate that men use quite a lot of condoms, women interviewed for this book reported how few men were prepared to use them for more than a couple of occasions, while others disliked what it did to their sex life. 'It's like making love with rubber gloves on,' was how one woman put it.

But although only 50 per cent of couples apparently use contraceptives when they first make love, and a remarkable number of young girls have very hazy notions of just when and how conception takes place – 'I thought you got one free go before you could get pregnant' were the woeful words of a pregnant teenager – most couples having sex regularly do use contraception most or all of the time.

Even when used properly contraceptives have a failure rate and this accounts for a certain number of the pregnancies which end in abortion. Isabel Allen, taking samples from different areas of the country of women who had become pregnant, found that 67 per cent of women in the south had been using contraceptives when they became pregnant, and 45 per cent in the north.[7] A study of women who had abortions in the Camden area of London found that two-thirds of the sample of 180 women interviewed said they were using contraceptives around the time they became pregnant, although some of them not as thoroughly and efficiently as they might have been.[8]

Dr Ashton, surveying 308 women asking for terminations in the Wessex region, found that just 25 per cent of the patients blamed contraception failure for their pregnancy.[9] The sheath was found, in Dr Ashton's study, to be the least reliable method. A good number of women talking to us blamed their pregnancy on a broken sheath. In the case of the cap, incorrect positioning or unwillingness to use spermicidal gel or cream can lead to failure. Pill failure may occur if the brand is changed, if it is taken erratically, or if it is used when a woman has some kind of gastric illness which means the chemicals are not properly absorbed. The IUD too has a 3 per cent failure rate.

Women tend to feel guilty and a failure if their contraception fails. Wendy put it like this: 'I felt somehow as though I had done something wrong when I got pregnant without wanting too. I'd been using a cap but I suppose occasionally I had skimped on applying the stuff, but really I made a big effort. But I was the one who was seen to have slipped up.' Lola, mother of three children, had a baby of just six months when she got pregnant:

> I was on the mini pill and I was breastfeeding my baby, so I really couldn't believe it. My strongest feeling was of failing, failing to prevent the horrid situation I had to face, from occurring.
>
> I think women do feel very responsible in life for making things all right, for getting life worked out, and getting pregnant when you don't want it is really not getting it right.

Some women do not use contraception. They come in for a good deal of criticism when unplanned pregnancies occur because it is women who are expected to cope with contraception over a long time. Indeed, there are men who simply assume their partner is doing so and do not bother to check, let alone offer to take the responsibility. Others do offer but after discussion the couple decide that female contraception is preferable.

Joan was prescribed a cap by her doctor, and when she became pregnant he admitted it had not been the best choice: 'I found out after two months with my boyfriend that I was pregnant. I was told then that, as a single parent, who really couldn't cope with another child, I shouldn't have been given it. But they tell you that afterwards.'

Nor is contraception always used. Indeed, Dr Ashton found that 45 per cent of his sample had not used contraceptives and other research has shown similar results. Isabel Allen has identified three groups of women who, she says, became pregnant as a result of not using precautions or using them intermittently.

They were very young girls, often under 16, who were having infrequent or unexpected intercourse. Women who were divorced or separated, who had often been regular users of contraception but were not using anything at the time of conception, and a small group of women over 40 who thought they might be menopausal.

Whatever the reason, when things go wrong women are the ones who are generally blamed and judged and who in turn blame and judge themselves. Men, equally implicated by their actions, are rarely criticized in the way women are for wayward fertility, pleasure or because they were 'caught out'.

3. Making the Decision

I'd never thought about abortion. It was something which happened to other people, to certain 'types' – you know, the promiscuous, kids, unstable people, but not to me. And there I was pregnant and having to think about it, having to weigh up whether I could cope with a kid I had not planned, I had no place for in life, or whether I could face abortion. (Gail)

I was married with two very young daughters when I got pregnant because of a broken sheath. My husband was livid and told me to get rid of it or he would divorce me and not pay maintenance for the child should I have it. I kept conjuring up pictures of being left alone with three children, unable to work, living in poverty and I also imagined my husband going off with another woman and being happy with her while I would be alone at nights. So although I had never envisaged abortion I allowed myself to be bullied into this decision. (Laura)

My boyfriend and I were at university together when I got pregnant. We talked over what to do but he did not offer to marry me so that we could keep the child and bring it up in a family. So I felt very clear that my only choice was to have an abortion because I believe every child has – or should have – the right to be brought up in a secure family. (Joanne)

We have a daughter, a lovely little girl who we love very much. But I found after having her that I didn't like motherhood much, the whole business bored me and I can't say I had strong maternal feelings. So when I found

I was pregnant I was horrified and absolutely clear that I
didn't want it. And the decision to have an abortion was
not a problem. It seemed very clearly a choice between
allowing this tiny organism to continue and take over my
life, or allowing myself to prevent it growing so that I
could continue leading the life I wish. I know people say
that's selfish, but I don't see it that way. We allow death
on the roads, death by smoking, as a society we don't
make much fuss about old people suffering and
sometimes dying from cold, malnutrition or just misery.
Yet when it comes to abortion and the idea of a life
which is still so unformed being stopped, a lot of
morality and sentimentality comes gushing out. (Lisa)

The decision to have an abortion is terrifying. I felt split
in two and I still haven't properly come to terms with it.
I didn't feel I had any other choice at the time, but I
couldn't go through it again. (Mary)

Women decide to have abortions for very different reasons,
and from very different perspectives. There are women who
are quite clear in their minds that choosing abortion is a
reasonable, morally acceptable decision. There are women
who see a foetus of a few weeks as no more than a bundle of
tissues and getting rid of it poses no dilemma. Others can
comfortably accept that they have the right to remove an
organism created by their bodies, within their bodies, but
which does not fit into their own fully fledged and functioning lives. There are women who argue that as long as we live
on an overcrowded globe where all kinds of human suffering as well as death are the fate of so many people because
there is no place, no support for them, preventing a foetus
becoming a viable person cannot be wrong.

For other women, abortion is an issue of life and death in
which they must pitch the seeming impossibility of having
and taking responsibility for a child against the right of that

potential child to live. There are women who have supported abortion without much thought, in theory, who find when confronted with an urgent, subjective choice that there is no simplicity in the idea of ending a life which is growing in their bodies. There are women who already have children, whose circumstances make another seem intolerable, yet the anguish they feel at the idea that they must take charge of preventing a child they can visualize so well from being, is appalling and enduring.

And in between these very different feelings about a personal abortion lie a variety of other less extreme but often conflicting and ambivalent feelings.

The picture that emerges from the interviews done for this book resembles a painting-by-numbers chart, with so many different shades and textures. There is no way, having heard the voices, that the processes women (and some men) have been through in deciding to end an unplanned pregnancy, can be lumped together or used to prove a particular political point about abortion.

Yet that is, generally, how abortion is treated. It is an issue which arouses heated, angry passions and which is generally discussed from two polarized moral, political standpoints: the anti-abortion and the pro-choice. Both sides consider the other to be subversive, invidious and hellbent on controlling the behaviour of women. And the entrenched, opposing arguments, which are battled out in the political arena, make abortion appear simple in a way that women, individually, do not experience it.

The pro-choice lobby, called 'pro-abortion' by their opponents, reject this label and point out that wishing for women to have choice in a situation where there appears, to them, no viable alternative is not the same as liking abortion. They hold, broadly, that women have the right to decide what happens to their conceptions, their bodies, their lives. It is especially important that it be a *woman's* choice, given the number of men who believe that childcare

is a job for the women – a view voiced by Patrick Jenkin
when Secretary of State for Social Services in the Thatcher
government: 'I don't think mothers have the same right to
work as fathers. If the good Lord had intended us to have
equal rights to go out to work, he wouldn't have created
men and women. These are biological facts: young children
depend upon their mothers.' The pro-choice answer is that
if women are so intimately tied to children, so inevitably
required to care for them, then it is essential that they be
able to make the ultimate choice about whether to take on
all that is entailed in nurturing and raising a child.

On the other side, the anti-abortionists, with their focal
organizations the Society for the Protection of the Unborn
Child (SPUC) and LIFE, which offers a counselling and
housing service for pregnant women, take the line that it is
the rights of the child which are of paramount importance
and that abortion is wrong, except in cases such as ectopic
pregnancy where the life of both mother and child is in
danger. With a compelling but deceptive simplicity, anti-
abortionists classify abortion as a human rights issue, argu-
ing that life and therefore human rights begin at conception. This means, they say, that ending the dependent but
potentially viable life of the foetus is no more morally
acceptable than child murder.

This argument is far easier to accept than abortion can
ever be. Who does not feel better about the idea of a new life
being nurtured and brought to fruition than that it should
be terminated at its fragile beginning? A great many of the
women who go on to terminate would share the feelings of
Antonia Hopkins at SPUC that 'abortion is profoundly
disturbing'. To the argument that the mother's life is as
important as the foetus's right to existence, that the circumstances in which she finds herself can endanger at a
fundamental level the quality of her life, possibly the lives
of a family she already has, and perhaps the life of the child,
the anti-abortionists answer that this is unfortunate

but does not justify abortion.

It can be seen, then, how deeply opposed the two sides in the abortion argument are. Both claim a feminist perspective – the pro-choice lobby because they support the woman, the anti-abortionists because they say abortion does not solve women's problems, that they are pressured into it and that they suffer enormously as a result. But to many people going through the experience of an abortion, the campaigning arguments do not get to grips with the ambivalence and uncertainty they feel. The simplicity of the arguments may be reassuring for those who need not question and challenge them in relation to their own lives, and a single focus may be necessary when making a political point, but such simplicity rarely exists for women who find themselves with an unwanted pregnancy.

Sula, an Asian girl born and brought up in London, became pregnant by a boyfriend who was in the middle of his studies, living at home and with no way to support a family.

> I had always condemned everyone who had an abortion. To me it was callous and I felt they became pregnant so they should live by their mistakes. But the tables turned when I found myself pregnant by my boyfriend who really didn't want the baby. I knew what a terrible smear it would be on his family to have an illegitimate child, and what a start to adult life it would be for him if he had to give up studying to look after me and a baby. So I too became callous.

May, married but not particularly happily with two young daughters, lives in a small house in the north of England and works part-time to supplement her husband's small income. At the time she became pregnant he was investing the little money they had in a business venture (which later failed).

> My husband was furious and would not even talk about

the idea of another baby. I pleaded with him that if I could have the child then I would be sterilized afterwards as three children would have been more than my ration but nothing I could say would persuade him.

I had never imagined having an abortion, I'd always thought I couldn't do that although I had believed in it being available for desperate girls who may be forced into going to a back-street abortionist. But there I was feeling there was no alternative because I knew my husband meant it when he said he would leave me if I didn't get rid of the baby and I couldn't face the idea of being alone, in poverty, trying to bring up three children.

Joan is in her early twenties and has one child by a relationship of a few years ago. When she got pregnant by a new boyfriend she felt devastated.

The idea of having two children, illegitimate, by different fathers was obviously not very good. I think, socially, you are allowed one mistake but with two you are labelled irresponsible, a tart – all that stuff. So that affected me quite a lot but if the dad had been keen I think I would have thought much harder about having the baby.

But he has always said he doesn't want children. He has a very low opinion of himself and is convinced that any child he has will be as 'bad' as he is. He just went into a black depression when I told him and he wouldn't discuss it. And although perhaps it sounds strange, I loved him a lot and wanted to stay with him, wanted to build the relationship up. He was good with my daughter too which was obviously important.

So I weighed up all these things and I have always believed in the right of abortion, that women must have the choice, so that wasn't a dilemma. But the thing which made me unhappy is that I get a lot of pleasure from my little girl, I do love kids and want more and it seemed awfully sad that this just didn't seem to be possible.

Meg:

My parents split up when I was little and me Mum brought me up on her own. She worked and made quite good money but she felt very trapped by me. I can remember her shouting at me once, 'I can't ever go out or have fun because I have to be a bloody childminder.' It was the only time she said it but I felt it a lot, that she really wished she didn't have me.

I got pregnant at 18 and although the boy was quite keen on the idea of my having it, and he did say he wanted to marry me, I knew I didn't want to. It wasn't a romance that was going to last; we fought a lot and had talked several times about ending it and I very much felt I was growing out of him.

So there I was all set to get myself into the same situation as my Mum and I didn't want that. I didn't want it for me and I didn't want it for the child because I know how much I suffered as a kid. And when I have kids I want to give them a really great childhood. I think it's really irresponsible to have a child when you don't feel you can offer it that.

Joanne's partner of several years discussed the pregnancy with her, but both agreed it was not the right time to have a child. She, more than he, was convinced of this.

I did wonder about adoption. I know that is the more humane choice and a good one to make at a time when so many couples want babies. But I just didn't feel I could face going through the pregnancy. However sure I was I didn't want a child, I think it would have been really traumatic to feel it growing, to form a relationship with it, then give it away. I'm not that virtuous a person.

The decision-making period is a time at which women must face an issue of life and death. Many find they must confront their personal morality, perhaps face a conflict with religious beliefs. For some women it is the most important decision they have been obliged to make alone. For however sympathetic and supportive the man involved may be, the experience cannot be the same for him. Fiona expressed this feeling:

> The decision to have the pregnancy terminated was the biggest decision we had ever had to make in our lives. We shared our feelings and talked a lot. We had no-one else to share it with so we kept it to ourselves.
>
> We looked at everything and came up with the conclusion it wouldn't have anything to come into the world to. We weren't married, we weren't ready for marriage. I was at college, Rob was on a government training scheme, there was no room at either of our houses and we were obviously penniless.
>
> We talked it over a lot and shed a lot of tears together and he couldn't have been more caring, more involved but even so I felt quite alone. It was my body, I had to have the abortion; I had to be the one to actually arrange it all.

There are very few circumstances in which we are obliged to face the issue of life or death in a context where we have choice and control and where, if we opt for life, it is a personal commitment to another human being for many years. People facing the idea of taking a life in wars have spoken of the trauma it inflicts – and in wars at least corporate morality is on your side. However, for a woman choosing abortion, the decision is hers and her partner's alone and it does not have the overall moral approval of society.

The parallel between abortion and taking a life in wars is sensitively described by Sara Maitland in an anthology of Christian writings.[10] She says:

In the light of lived experience, how can anyone describe the unborn child as 'innocent' given the teachings of the Church in other areas about the sanctity of human life. Just as it is permissible to kill another individual (say a conscript soldier, or a lunatic) who, though personally guiltless, is endangering either individual or societal life; so it should be possible to admit that for many women a baby is not innocent – 'devoid of harm'. A child may actually and directly threaten a woman's health, well-being, material and social environment, sanity, to say nothing of life, liberty and the pursuit of happiness.

In some women's lives a child is exactly as innocent as a shoal of hungry piranha fish. Ethically we must take a line which either unites an anti-abortionist stance with a complete pacifism or we must permit relativist situationalist concerns to inform our conduct within the whole 'value of human life' discussions.

In saying this, Sara Maitland acknowledges that a moral absolute does not exist in the abortion issue. As the women spoken to demonstrate, time and again their morality may make abortion seem abhorrent and wrong, but their circumstances make having a child seem so impossibly problematic that they select abortion as the lesser of two evils. Such reasoned compassion must surely be helpful to women feeling distressed about a choice which, to quote Sara Maitland again, is 'a decision of despair; it is a grievous pain for a woman to face the fact that the world is intolerable for her and her child.' Yet too often those who could most easily, most effectively offer her compassion do the opposite.

Doctors, who are so often the first people to learn about a woman's unplanned pregnancy and whose relationship to a woman permits them to offer non-judgemental counselling and care, too frequently do the reverse. Fiona remembers: 'I had an afternoon off work to see the gynaecologist at a local hospital. I explained to him that we had been using condoms and one broke and he turned away, and said very abruptly that it was a highly unlikely story. He might as well have called me a liar.' When Elizabeth asked her GP about abortion he turned to her and said: 'Even if I help you, don't ever imagine that I approve. Just remember there are thousands of people out there who think as I do that a woman who has an abortion has something irreparably bad in her character.' Connie, a divorcee in her mid-thirties, got pregnant after a brief affair which she had ended when she found she was pregnant.

I was quite clear in my mind that abortion was the only right and sensible solution. I went to see the doctor who made it clear from the beginning that he didn't agree with abortion. He told me I was trying to fix the law to suit myself and that all these women killing babies was a sign of the times.

Then he asked why I wouldn't have it and give it up for adoption as so many people want babies. Well, I know that and in an ideal world it would be great if every unwanted baby could be dealt with that way, but things aren't set up to make it possible. I had a job I'd have lost for a start if I had done that. Besides I don't see my role as providing that sort of social service.

All the same, the things he said got to me; I began to feel very upset and uneasy, then fortunately – I think – I got angry. I asked him if he had a private clinic and if he did terminations and he said yes. Well, that made me feel a lot better because it was such appalling hypocrisy.

Understandably, such attitudes do not make it easy for women to work out, according to their own circumstances, their own values and conscience, what really is the best thing to do. That we are aware abortion is a matter of life and death seems right. If women are going to have the right to make the choice about something so fundamentally problematic as abortion, confronting what it is really about and taking responsibility for that seems essential. We have to face the fact that a conception does lead to a living organism with the potential to become a child, that it is not just a mass of cells. A refusal to acknowledge reality is not helpful to a woman in contemplating the choice facing her. Nor is ducking the issue helpful to those women who do see this reality, the gravity of what they are doing, and who grieve over what they feel they must do.

But to recommend a reasoned recognition of the implications of the abortion decision is not to support the kind of crude propaganda which is put out by the anti-abortion groups, which see no place for reason or sensitivity in their desire to convince us that abortion is evil. A LIFE advertisement showed, at the end of 1985, the minute feet of an aborted foetus with the words, 'These feet were made for walking'; another carries a picture of foetuses with the words, 'Six unborn children killed under the 1967 Abortion Act'. Yet more emotive and distressing was the film made and shown in Britain in 1985 by American doctor Bernard Nathanson, a one-time abortionist, turned zealous supporter of SPUC.

This film purported to show the suffering and screaming of a foetus as an abortion is performed. The film was subsequently criticized and its credibility and accuracy challenged by doctors in Britain and America. But an attempt to undo the pain inflicted on women by such a film can never be so effective as the graphic images of a tormented foetus which the film evokes. It cannot remove from women's minds the idea that they are inflicting on their own conception a level of pain and distress which, in fact, it seems probable only a far more developed human can experience. It brings to mind the publication soon after the 1967 Act of a notorious book called *Babies for Burning* which set out to do an in-depth report on the workings of the Act and was packed full of hideous case histories of evil abortionists, wretched, exploited women who grievously regretted their abortions. It was only after some in-depth reporting by the *Sunday Times* (and others) that the book was proved to be pure fiction.

In the context of such propaganda – the rantings of magazines like the *Plain Truth*, equating abortion with sterilization in Nazi Germany, and the parading outside abortion clinics by anti-abortion groups with enlarged photographs of foetuses – women are understandably upset. And that is taken by anti-abortionists as proof that abortion is the wrong choice, a choice they have been pressured into by today's 'abortion culture'; by parents, partners, etc., who do not want a child; by the pro-choice lobby. In this invasive propaganda, as well as in the expressed desire to have the abortion law repealed, there is an implicit belief on the part of anti-abortionists that they have the right to set themselves up as guardians of the nation's morality and to make it as unpleasant as possible for women to choose an option which is now within the law. Antonia Hopkins at SPUC explains that they see the abortion law as, on the one hand, brutalizing, in that it allows a society to dispose of life because it is inconvenient (and she too invokes 'the memory of Hitler'); and on the other, she explains that it is very difficult to get the kind of reforms they would like to see, which would make life easier for women who do go ahead with unplanned pregnancies, as long as abortion is an option. Given the problems that women with an unplanned pregnancy face, it would seem that the crude, strident tone of the anti-abortionist propaganda is far from helpful. In fact, it can be very painful to women deciding on whether or not to have an abortion.

But while morality is certainly utterly central to the abortion dilemma, the issue is further complicated by physiology. As a woman becomes more pregnant her body adjusts to the condition, hormones affect the way she feels; many women experience an unexpected surge of maternal feeling, they become acutely aware of their fecundity. And while they may wish to cast off the unpleasant symptoms of nausea, vomiting, lethargy, etc., many women may equally feel more and more loath to abruptly end the drive to remain pregnant, powerfully imposed by nature. Marge recalls the feeling well:

> I felt very very aware of the foetus – the baby as it seemed to me – inside me. I had quite a long wait before I could get my abortion and I thought endlessly about the baby: I visualized it in me and I remember vividly whenever I was alone in a room I felt as though I had company.
>
> It made having the abortion very painful, but there wasn't anything else to be done that I could see.

In the early days of the pro-choice lobby's battle to make a woman's right to choose legal, there was no place for admitting ambivalences, contradictions. To admit these was to risk providing ammunition for the opposition who might capitalize on an admission of ambivalence as proof that abortion had been a wrong choice.

But as feminism moves on to a more discursive stand on a number of women's issues, abortion too is being re-examined as a subject where women's feelings are important alongside their rights. This is a perspective Kathleen McDonnell has taken on in writing *Not an Easy Choice*, a feminist reappraisal of the abortion issue.[11] Her reasons for doing so were precisely that she felt that the pro-choice politics which argue a woman's right to choose and assume this is enough, fail to allow the truth of women's feelings to be expressed. She writes:

> The book is the product of a very personal reexamination of my own thinking on abortion. At many points in this process, I felt a bit like a feminist heretic, attending pro-choice rallies and marches while secretly harbouring thoughts and feelings that seemed to clash

with what I saw as the official 'line' on abortion.
Gradually I found myself coming back to a basic feminist
truth: that our 'politics' cannot afford to be divorced
from our authentic feelings, no matter how vague or
contradictory they may seem. Our real task is to search
out and find ways to reconcile the two.

Marlene's experience makes the same point:

I decided to have an abortion, but I didn't like myself for
doing it, I didn't feel good about it and the fact that I was
exercising my right to choose did not heal the pain I felt
at having ended a life.

But when I tried to talk with friends who are involved
with the abortion battle, as I have always been, about
this they were really unsympathetic. One woman got
very cross and said to me, 'It's not on to talk like this,
you'll be joining the anti-abortionists next.'

And I found myself feeling afterwards that this hard
line is really cruel; it's absolutely not about sisters
working towards a good world for each other.

It is not easy for women to realize that there may not be a
clear-cut 'right' solution, that happy endings, the perfect
answer, the doubt-free denouement is more often the stuff
of fiction than of real life. And particularly so with a matter
which delves so deep into our cultural and biological
nature. So while there are certainly some women who feel
quite undisturbed in the choice to terminate what Germaine Greer refers to as 'fertilization . . . a very nominal
beginning',[12] there are far more women who experience no
such certainty, whose decisions are made in the best way
they can find, and do not provide the wonderful clarity of a
choice which is 100 per cent morally and practically right.

This is a dilemma which Janice Bumstead who, during
her time as Director of the Marie Stopes Clinic, spoke with
hundreds of women making the decision to have an abortion, well understands:

It is painful and dreadful in many ways to face the fact that you have the power to decide whether life shall continue or not, and it is apalling that we have so little way of allowing women to mourn their choice.

But I think it is vital that they do face up to this and resolve it for themselves before having the abortion. When talking to women I used to say to them that there is not a 100 per cent right or wrong in this. You will make a choice which seems the best one under the circumstances and you will have to live with that and resolve it. But looking for a perfect answer is hopeless. How can it exist in a situation like this? I support the right of women to choose abortion because I know that for some women the alternative is too terrifying, too much to impose on her life.

That doesn't make me like it. I have seen abortions performed. I know exactly what it means and I understand very well that women who understand too may suffer. But still I think it can be the thing women must choose in certain circumstances even though it is clear they *will* suffer later. Then the suffering needs to be tackled.

It is easy to be punitive, but we need to recognize that as a society we do little to help the mother who has more children than she can cope with. Single mothers and those in poverty get very, very little support. And it is here that I take issue strongly with the anti-abortion supporters – if they feel so strongly about the value of life why don't they work towards trying to improve the circumstances of those who have children and find themselves in difficulties? Providing short-term housing as LIFE does is not enough. It may be a palliative for a short while but it isn't tackling the root difficulties these mothers have over many years.

4. Counselling and Support

It was the opportunity to talk with someone else that was so helpful. As you talk about things you become clearer in your own mind what you are thinking. The counsellor was really nice – she was a single mother. I thought maybe she would disapprove of abortion because she had a child, but she didn't. She said she really loved her daughter and was glad she had her, but that it was very hard doing it alone and financially it's really tough.

My circumstances were harder than hers because I'd also have had to give up work. But being able to talk very realistically like that was helpful. (Linda)

The counsellor at the private clinic was marvellous. She was the first person I'd been able to talk to. She was patient and kind without being patronizing and she just kept asking me questions – I never once felt she felt I should or shouldn't do it. They listened and gave me lots of time to just go on about it all. (Carol)

I had the termination with no counselling, no advice or help. Perhaps if we had had some advice I wouldn't have had the abortion, I don't know. But there seemed to be no support. I felt as if I had no answers to the problem, nor was getting any help, and in short this was the only way out.

At a time when you are worried, frightened, depressed, you need someone to give a little advice on alternatives, on what abortion entails and whether this is what you need and what is right for you. It is very difficult to think properly in this situation. (Jenny)

When women face the decision whether or not to have an abortion, finding someone neutral, supportive and willing to listen is enormously helpful. Professionals working in the field talk of how often women find it easier to come to terms with an abortion if they can feel confident that they have made the decision themselves, without panic or pressure.

Not surprisingly. It is a natural impulse for women from a very young age to seek out a friend, a relative, someone close to confide in when times are hard, when there is some crisis or dilemma to be coped with. Women seem to have a greater awareness of the value of this kind of sharing and sorting out than do many men. And the women's movement has done much to encourage women of all types and classes to get together to talk, exchange ideas, to share their dreams and dilemmas, their trials and traumas. Many women have found comfort and enlightenment through coming together and breaking down restraints and taboos on intimate subjects.

Yet when it comes to abortion many women find they cannot go out and seek help. Women who would spontaneously discuss with those around them – friends, lovers, relatives – issues of intimacy and anxiety, find that when faced with the profoundly painful and complicated decision concerning abortion, it is impossible to do so. Abortion remains a taboo, a subject which touches too closely on the fusing of a woman's sexuality and maternal nature, the small core of power she maintains in our patriarchal culture. So many women find they dare not talk to others for fear of the shock and condemnation it might bring. Often they do not feel entitled to go out and ask for help and support.

> Sue: I just held the knowledge of what I was going to do inside me. I didn't dare think hard about it because I was afraid I might break down, cry, give away the secret. I

just couldn't talk to any of the women friends I have
because I felt sure they would disapprove, they would
see me as an evil woman for killing a child. There was
nobody around who I felt would be able to let me talk
without judging me.

Lisa: I really wanted the baby but my boyfriend didn't
and when I tried to persuade him he became very angry
and so I knew there really wasn't any choice because I
couldn't have managed alone. Once I had arranged the
abortion I was so sad and unhappy and I had no-one to
tell as John said I couldn't tell anyone, no-one must
know. I only had myself and the thoughts which were
flowing through my mind and I couldn't sort them out at
all.

Janice: I have a close friend I always talk to about
everything really. But she is quite religious and I felt sure
that she would just say I shouldn't go ahead with an
abortion and that would have been very hard. I wasn't
feeling good about it anyway and I really just wanted
someone who would say it was all right, I could do what
seemed the right thing to me. I felt very lonely; I think
something like that makes you very aware of how
difficult it is doing something which goes against
society's code of practice.

Mora: I still don't know if I made the right decision; I did
it so alone. I went to my GP who was kindly enough but
didn't really talk to me, she just said, yes, she would
recommend me for abortion. I wish she had given me the
chance to talk a bit about it all but I suppose she was in
a hurry. And I couldn't tell my Mum, I knew she would
be that mad and my Dad would have kicked me out so I
just kept very quiet and when Mum said how poorly I
looked I told her I had a dose of flu. So I bottled up all

the questions, all the things which worried me and went through it like a zombie. And like I said I still don't know if it was the right thing. I still feel terrible about it a lot of the time.

Jean: I'm a social worker and people get the impression I'm very worked out, very sure of what I do. So even though I was screaming inside nobody realized it and that made it hard to talk to anyone. I didn't have a very close friend or parent around and I didn't want to tell anyone I didn't feel close to.

The feelings of these women are very different from those of Ruth who had a close friend with whom she was able to spend time sharing feelings:

My friend had a small child and had chosen not to have an abortion when she got pregnant, so I did feel apprehensive about talking with her, but I guess I know her well enough to know she is not going to assume I should make the same choice. And when I told her that I was pregnant, that I didn't know what to do about it, she just said, 'Let's talk about the choices you have. They all have advantages and disadvantages.' I really blessed her for that because she was recognizing that I did have abortion in mind and she was saying it's okay, you can make that decision if you want.

We talked a long long time and I listened very carefully to what she had to say about the delight she gets as a mother, but then she discussed the enormous change it makes in your life, the fact that if you have to have a child you have got to be even more sure it's right than if you have an abortion. And that was helpful, really helpful, because it clarified the issue for me. I wasn't choosing a bad solution versus a good one if I went for abortion, I was actually doing something more honest and better than having a kid I really didn't want. Then I felt okay, that I could go ahead. And I still bless her for that. I don't know that I would have coped so well if she hadn't made the reason for abortion seem so clear.

Morag had a neighbour who saw her when she was vomiting one morning and guessed.

She just said, 'I suppose you're pregnant. How do you feel about it?' Just like that. She's not someone I'd have told; I'd have felt sure she would be very against abortion; well I think a lot of people are, aren't they? So then I said, 'Well yes, I am, and it's a bit of a muddle,' and she said very matter-of-factly, 'I had a termination three years ago. I didn't like doing it but there was nothing for it and it's all right now. I feel all right now.'
    So then I could tell her that's what I was thinking of and she was that helpful telling me all about it, telling me which doctor in our practice to see and she visited me when I went in. It was a real surprise finding her so nice about it all.

Women who have a good relationship with their mothers often turn thankfully to them for help and advice when they discover pregnancy. Peggy's comment is typical: 'I was so glad my Mum is a really loving person. She was shocked at first but she then just agreed with me that having the babe wasn't right and she helped me a lot by holding me very tight and talking about the life I would have ahead.'
    There are, of course, mothers who are too shocked, too disgusted at finding their daughters pregnant to be able to support and help them. There are mothers who do not 'want the neighbours to know'; mothers who cannot accept a daughter's sexuality and therefore reject her rather than offering help and support.

Lesley: I live with my Mum in a council house and Dad's out of work so I just knew she would be mad with me if she knew I was pregnant. She has often said how awful she thinks abortion is so I couldn't have told her I was thinking of that. But I knew too that having a baby at home would have been just awful. So I had to get a friend to help me go to a clinic.

Brenda: My mother just isn't the sort of person you can talk to about anything intimate. She's always been very distant about anything to do with sex or emotional feelings and I just know she wouldn't have been able to help me in my troubles, so I didn't say anything and she never guessed.

Sara: I just know my Mum would be furious and Dad's always said he'd throw us out if we got pregnant. It happened to my sister and he did, so it's not an idle threat. I haven't anywhere to live and although there were times when I really wanted to talk to her I knew I couldn't.

More often, judging by the interviews done for this book, mothers, in particular, end up being supportive and helpful to their daughters. After the initial burst of anger, the first feelings of hurt, they often become very helpful and supportive.

Annette: I wasn't going to tell my Mum because I was scared. But then she guessed because I was very pale and off my food, and one day she came into the bathroom and saw my swollen breasts and she knew straight away. She was that mad for about three days and could hardly talk to me, but then she came into my room and said, 'So what are we going to do? Are you going to have it or what?' And then I knew that however cross she was, I could talk to her about it. I was that relieved because I love my Mum and she was so good to me through the abortion.

Mary Brunswick, who has worked for several months in a private abortion clinic outside London, had ample opportunity to chat with the mothers of girls who were coming in and she saw the caring they offered their daughters, often hiding their own strain and worry in order to be supportive.

The mums would come in when their daughters were due for admission and you could see on their faces that they were coping with it all and feeling really quite stressed themselves. But they were great with the girls, very strong and kind. One or two confided to me that they had been very scared what the dads would say and that they had felt angry at being put in a position of having to keep secrets, but they all felt, ultimately, that helping their daughters was the most important thing.

Young women who can turn to their mothers are lucky. For older women, women separated from their families, the problem may be how to find someone to talk to. Clearly a friend is good if a woman has someone she trusts, but others would like somebody more anonymous and many have talked of the lack of counselling available at the time they most want it.

Not every woman who bottles up her feelings and copes alone with the experience of abortion suffers. Women who feel very sure in their minds about what they are doing, who have no doubts about being entitled to make this choice, and those who do not feel guilty at the idea of preventing a potential child from being born often seem to cope perfectly well.

Much of the recorded material on abortion deals with the situation of those women who do not cope well, although doctors and counsellors talk of a good many women who feel they have made a reasonable and right decision, as did Barbara: 'I knew a child would be a disaster at this moment in life. In an overpopulated, under-resourced world where we allow plenty of people to die, I cannot feel bad about preventing another life coming into being when there really isn't a space for it.' Or Gemma:

> I would have loved another kid but we couldn't have afforded it, so I knew I had to go through with an abortion. I didn't let myself dwell on the idea of little babies and foetuses and all that. I just got myself to the doctor early and luckily he's a good guy who fixed it up quick. So I went in, took a good book and my husband took me there and wished me luck and that was that. We didn't talk about it afterwards because it was over and I'm not one to brood when I know something has to be done.

These women are fortunate in that they are able to allow themselves such certainty and peace of mind. For other women no such sureness can be reached and the professionals interviewed all agreed that, in these circumstances, it can be very destructive for a woman to go through the ordeal without a chance of exploring her feelings. Not being able to talk through feelings, to resolve them and come to terms with them before the operation, may mean that a woman does not face up to what she is doing until after the abortion is over. She may then feel devastated, she may not be able to assimilate the experience and she may then become very depressed. In the words of Peggy Wakelin, a founder of BPAS and senior counsellor:

> I regard counselling, whether it is done by a professional or by a friend, as allowing the woman to listen to herself. And while not all women need this, by any means, for some women it is the only way to come to terms with what must be done.
>
> I don't think many women make the wrong decision about abortion, but that doesn't mean they won't suffer. And when I talk to women I tend to stress that sadness and grief is a normal response to abortion, but that it is also possible to cope with it.

Yet although counsellors who work both privately and within the state sector are convinced of the value of non-judgemental counselling for women approaching abortion (and the DHSS issued a circular in 1977 recommending that every woman should be offered it), there is no provision for counselling in the Abortion Act.

Of course, measuring the value of counselling which depends for its effectiveness on both the counsellor and the client and which must be influenced considerably by how open and honest the client feels able to be, may be difficult. But as Gillian Clarke, in her investigation into feelings about the abortion services,[13] points out, little research has been done to try to find out the effects of counselling. Isabel Allen, looking for reactions to counselling, found that they tended to be positive.[14] She reports that 86 per cent of women who had talked to Pregnancy Advisory Bureaux counsellors, found them helpful. And in her study women quite often expressed a wish for further counselling.

When women do decide they want to talk to someone, who is the appropriate person to try first? There are various people who, in theory, can offer talk, information, advice and support. Very often the first person the woman turns to is her GP. In a number of cases GPs are helpful and kindly and will talk through the situation with a woman, then suggest she go away and think for a couple of days before making a decision. Others let the woman know they are prepared to help in whatever choice she makes – there is no doubt that women who have encountered this supportive approach in their doctors have found it helpful.

> Carolyn: He was good. He told me that he would do all he could to help me if I was sure I wanted an abortion, but then he asked me questions about me and my boyfriend and how I would cope if I had it. Things like that. In a way that was good because it forced me to look at the options. I was grateful to him because he was really kind.

Sue: My GP was pleasant but she was obviously worried that I really didn't understand what I was doing, what I might feel. I have a five-year-old son and she talked to me about the fact I might well feel loss and sadness afterwards, that I might imagine what it would have been like to have another child. I think she was right to do that because I think it *is* necessary to think through those issues and not just pretend they don't exist.

Then she said go away for a couple of days and come back and let me know what you think. I felt she had helped me.

Dr Maggie Helliwell sees the doctor's role at this early stage as crucial in allowing the woman to feel strong about her choice, and she is convinced that doctors who criticize and are judgemental, who 'want to control women, make them fit their image of good passive women' are often responsible for the pain and conflict women feel after the event. She says:

It is known in our area that I am sympathetic to abortion so most women know this when they come in and if they don't I let it be known. But I would never suggest an abortion. I consider it very important that, at this stage, there is no pressure put on a woman to have an abortion or to have the baby. The point is for me to give her the opportunity to talk about why she is asking for a termination, why she has mixed feelings about what to do, if that is the case.

In fact in my experience most women know what they want. When they come in they are looking to me for tacit approval. If I feel they are uncertain then I try to let them talk while knowing I will help them get the abortion if they want, but equally that I have no vested interest in their doing so. I also say that they can change their mind at any time up to going into the operating theatre.

When there are people who seem uncertain I send

them away if there's time to think a bit longer, and I have had cases where the women don't come back, which is fine. I feel I've given them the space to make that choice but without anxiety about whether they can or can't get an abortion.

I feel quite confident that after this process women do feel able to make their own decision even if they haven't already done so, and it makes me very angry when I hear the anti-abortionists or members of the medical profession saying women are pressurized into abortion by evil doctors. It's so demeaning to women.

In her research into counselling,[15] Isabel Allen notes that professionals often talk of GPs as the best people to give counselling, but because GPs are a very mixed bunch, the kind of help women get is very varied and ranges from such remarks as, 'I've counselled this woman but she still wants an abortion ... ' and, 'How can you think because you have got yourself into this mess it's right to kill a baby,' and very routine formalities, to doctors such as Dr Helliwell who recognize the importance of providing the patient with a chance to work through the situation.

The level of 'counselling' received from a GP also varied considerably depending on whether the abortion was NHS or private. Allen notes that a far higher percentage of women going to private abortion clinics or the charities felt able to discuss their situation and get sympathetic help, than those on the NHS.

The other person in a unique position to offer comfort, help and reassurance if he or she wishes to give it is the consultant who may be going to perform the operation, who knows the hospital and the procedure well. Yet consultants do not have a good record for offering this kind of care. Only 19 per cent of the women in Isabel Allen's study found talking with the consultant helpful and the majority of these were married women. Young women frequently get little sympathy, and sometimes experience consultants as highly critical.

> I wanted to ask the gynaecologist what was going to happen but I couldn't do anything but weep after he'd called me a stupid, immoral child who would have to suffer for my mistake.

> He gave me the most painful internal I've ever had and scarcely spoke except to say how much he disapproved of abortion. I felt so disgusting and dirty after that.

Meg, an older woman who got pregnant as a result of a brief, unexpected affair became angry rather than upset with the consultant she saw.

> I saw this man and it was the most awful experience. He said I was trying to twist the law to suit myself and that he didn't believe in abortion. It made me mad so I said to him, 'Do you have a private clinic?' and he said yes, he did, so I just said, 'So you make money out of abortion yet you criticize me,' and then he got very angry and said, 'Even if you paid me I wouldn't see you again,' so I had to start all over again trying to get my abortion.

The people to whom a good many women do go for the chance to talk and to inform themselves are abortion counsellors and Isabel Allen in her study found that for pregnant women talking to one of these counsellors was more helpful than conversations with doctors, consultants or social workers. The reason for this is simple: counsellors trained to help women sort through their jumbled emotions and ambivalences, trained to listen and to allow women a neutral sounding board can frequently offer a kind of help that it is very difficult for people closer to the woman to give. And as pointed out earlier, the counsellor may also be the only person to whom the woman will disclose her secret.

So what is the role of counsellor when a woman, con-

templating abortion, goes for an appointment? Helena, a
senior counsellor with one of the large private charities,
says:

> To me the most important, fundamental thing is helping
> the woman decide whether she has a value system which
> will allow her to live with the knowledge that she has
> had an abortion afterwards. She needs to have thought
> about the implications of abortion, she needs to have
> considered what it has meant to her in the past. I quite
> often get women coming in who say, 'I've never agreed
> with abortion before but now it has happened to me I
> feel differently,' and those people need to be sure they
> really mean that, that they feel they can make the
> abortion experience part of their history.
>
> The anti-abortionists insist on saying that we
> persuade people to have abortions, they seem to think
> we actually want people to have abortions, but that just
> isn't true. We counsellors working for charities have
> nothing to gain by a woman having an abortion, and I
> take my job seriously enough to feel that it's very
> important the woman makes the best possible choice for
> her future good.

In counselling, women are not helped towards one or
other choice, rather they are encouraged to examine the
options while the counsellor guides them through this process, perhaps asking questions. Helena explains:

> There are plenty of women who come in quite clear in
> their minds what they want to do and with no real
> problem about it and usually I find they just want to seek
> approval for this attitude. But for other women it is a
> major upheaval. Plenty of women have gone through life
> without really making decisions for themselves – there's
> always been parents, boyfriends, husband – and
> suddenly they are faced with pregnancy and they realize

that really nobody else can make the decision for them. It is a very lonely time for women and no wonder they need to talk, they need support.

Counselling may also include filling out the picture of the woman's circumstances – how she became pregnant, whether she was using contraception, her attitude to the relationship – all of which can help a counsellor to find her way through the issues. Helena also believes in giving information about the abortion procedure so that the woman does not feel ignorant and scared when she is admitted. This is particularly important with young women and teenage girls who may have all sorts of terrifying ideas about what the abortion entails. Some, she says, arrive 'absolutely terrified because of what their GP has said, or if they have gone to LIFE, say, for a pregnancy test and have been told all sorts of horror stories.' She explains:

> We know how common an experience it is but of course a great many women don't realize this. They feel that they alone are actually the kind of person who contemplates killing a foetus; they feel the world can spot them as 'marked' women, that kind of thing, so part of the job is helping them realize how many women have to go through what they are going through. I know this can be very reassuring.

Another part of the counselling role, Helena feels, is to explain the abortion risks to women if they are worried. She says:

> There is no doubt that the risk of infertility is used by anti-abortionists to frighten women even though it appears to be very slight. They may also fear that there will be divine punishment preventing them conceiving, or that they will get a child with something wrong with it next time. It is very important that we allow those women to talk through their fears before they go for the

abortion, to understand how unfounded they are, rather than bottling them up and wondering and feeling bad for years after the operation.

Of course we can never make abortion a pleasant experience, but I honestly believe that counselling can prevent it from being a very traumatic one.

For women who go straight to a private clinic when they find they are pregnant, a counsellor may be the first person they meet while trying to come to terms with the abortion decision as well as trying to actually set it up. The Brook Advisory Clinics around the country tend to see young women, many of whom go to them first for advice, even though they may eventually go on to try to get an NHS abortion through their GPs. Teenagers, who are probably less used to facing and coping with crises than older women and those who already have families, may well be in a very emotional, upset state when they go for an interview. Caroline Bailey, senior counsellor at Brook, describes how many weep, are very muddled and upset in their ideas, and need a lot of time before they can begin to think rationally about what to do. Often enough the father of the child is behaving in a way which increases the distress and problems. This being so, a first appointment of up to three-quarters of an hour is allowed and women may return as often as they wish before making a decision. Caroline explains:

> We would never push a girl to decide she must have an abortion, but I do feel it essential to point out that the risks and the ordeal increase if the abortion is left until after three months. It is important that the girl has this information. But I would absolutely never push anyone towards making the decision to abort if she seemed truly uncertain and we would always give advice on ways of coping if she did go ahead and have the baby.
>
> People often ask why we don't counsel girls to have their babies and get them adopted, as a way of

preventing them going through the trauma of abortion and also to help offset the shortage of babies for adoption. Well, very very few girls feel they could go through with that.

Certainly that is how 18-year-old Cathy felt:

I got a pregnancy test done and when I broke down at the positive result, the nurse suggested I should have it adopted. She said that was the right thing to do, that I would feel better than if I got rid of it. Well, I did think about it but I like babies and I do want them some time, and I know so well that I just couldn't have gone through with it. Then I'd either have ended up a single mum living on social, or I'd have forced myself to give it away and I think I'd have suffered the rest of my life.

Kay, who has two children of her own, is appalled at the easy way adoption is suggested: 'I think giving a baby away when it has grown in you for all those months would tear you apart. I know it would destroy me.'

There are times with young people when Caroline Bailey believes that the emphasis of counselling must be to help them be very clear in their minds just what the decision means. She says: 'The point I make is that they must allow themselves time and space to think the thing through properly. If there's a supportive man then obviously it's sensible to talk with him, but still it is the girl who is going to have to go through with either abortion or coping with a baby and with the growing person for the rest of its life. They do need to face that.'

Anger is one of the emotions frequently displayed in counselling sessions – some women are then able to release the frustrations and resentments they have been building up. Caroline Bailey says: 'I spend a lot of time working through anger. I think it is a perfectly acceptable emotion, but it is not a useful emotion when it comes to making a decision like this. When a girl is in this state I really do try to see her two or three times before she comes to deciding.'

Counsellors see as clearly as anyone the different ways women cope with unplanned pregnancies and with making a decision about abortion. Caroline believes that for some the decision is evidently not particularly traumatic, and a point made by a number of counsellors is that it is important to realize that not all women do feel bad, remorseful, regretful, guilty about choosing an abortion. It is a point which Madelaine Simms, a long-time member of the abortion law reform movement, makes: 'Most women who apply for abortion nowadays [1977] do not feel that they are contemplating something intrinsically wicked or shameful, as many had been brought up to believe.'[16]

If one accepts that women do have the right to make this choice and to control their own fertility and biological destiny, there is no reason they should feel evil. Unless you believe absolutely that the destruction of a living organism is a sin, there can be situations in which an abortion is the best solution. Yet a great many women cannot or will not allow themselves to be so rational, for one effect of the abortion taboo is that it makes women feel obliged to suffer. They feel that they are inhuman, callous, uncaring creatures if they do not. Added to this, the woman 'capable' of abortion may well be labelled as a child hater, as someone lacking in 'natural' maternal instincts, all of which creates ambivalence and distress in how she assesses her options.

Unless she has a thorough and supportive discussion of all the pros and cons of the situation, a woman who has an abortion can experience very painful grief after the termination – a grief all the more painful for being repressed. For as Caroline Bailey says:

> So many women feel they are not entitled to express grief. Women who see abortion as bad, evil, may well feel that they have to suffer as a penance, that they may not

receive sympathy or compassion.

I honestly believe that talking it out first can and frequently does prevent depression and severe distress afterwards. That is not to say there will be no feelings of sadness or regret afterwards. There may well be these, but if a woman has found a way of coming to terms with what she is doing, feels she has made a decision in a clear state of mind, the chances are she will manage to cope with it.

5. Arranging the Abortion

Discussing the moral aspects of abortion is valuable in giving the issue a context, but for a woman who does not wish to have a child, the practical details of arranging an abortion are equally important. It requires considerable determination to get an abortion organized and for many women this a daunting task, one that requires energy and strength just when they at their lowest.

Joan: I delayed going to the doctor because I just didn't want to make abortion real. I had decided, in my mind, that it was best, but I knew that if I got my doctor's agreement then I would have to face up to what it would actually be like.

I know this can be read as being uncertain about what I was doing. Well, who can ever be 100 per cent certain, but I did see that having a baby was an act of cowardice, rather than an act of courage or love. I would have done it because I couldn't face the idea of going through an abortion, not because I felt the child should live. So I went to my doctor and luckily he was very kindly and helpful and accepted that I was the one who should decide whether it was right or not.

Meg: My boyfriend and I spent days discussing what to do. At nights we lay in bed and cried and I kept asking him to put his hands on my tummy because I wanted him to really *feel* that I was pregnant before I did what I knew I must and saw a doctor.

Brenda, married with two sons, was certain she did not want more children. She had had severe kidney pains during both pregnancies and had never completely recovered.

I had to come off the Pill because of my kidneys and the coil caused me a lot of pain so we used sheaths. Then one broke and I knew immediately I would be pregnant. There was no way I felt I could go through with having another child. My husband is a van driver and doesn't earn much; I was feeling unwell much of the time with my kidneys; my sons by this time were nine and thirteen and I had been able to start working to improve our finances.

So I felt very clear in my mind that these were good enough reasons for an abortion when I went to my doctor. But I had a shock. He told me flatly that because I was a married woman, living with my husband and family and reasonably young there wasn't the slightest chance that I would be able to have an abortion on the National Health.

I was shocked and really upset. Suddenly it seemed that not only did I have to face the unpleasant business of abortion, which I certainly didn't relish, but I was going to have to struggle to even get one. No amount of crying or pleading made any difference but in the end he did tell me about the Pregnancy Advisory Service.

Most women start by going to their GP because that seems the logical and appropriate thing to do and because we look to our doctors to help when we have health problems. But just over half the number of women who go on to have terminations do so privately. The reason a great many women make the decision to go private, a decision which often entails considerable financial difficulty, is that they cannot get a sympathetic, early abortion on the NHS.

For although the law permits abortion, it does not let the woman decide whether her circumstances 'justify' her choice. That judgement lies squarely with the medical profession whose members hold differing views on who should and should not have abortions. Some, such as Professor Peter Huntingford, a long-time champion of women's right to choose and architect of the day-care abortion centres, believes that women must be the ones to make the decision and that the role of the medical profession is only to support and help her in her choice. Others interpret the law very narrowly and will 'grant' abortions only to women who have strong medical reasons or who can clearly be seen to be in danger of mental illness if they have a baby.

So the woman going to see her GP for the first time cannot feel clear that at least she is asking for something which is her right, that she should be the person to work out the morality of the decision. Instead, she must go along hoping that her doctor will be sympathetic and that her reason for asking is good enough to persuade him (or her). What this means is that women find themselves struggling not only with the feelings they have about going through an abortion, but they must also worry about whether they have a strong enough case to 'convince' their doctor to allow an abortion. Mr John Lawson, consultant obstetrician at the Newcastle General Hospital and a doctor who is sympathetic and supportive to women wanting abortion, recalls:

> A woman came in to me very nervously, saying her husband was beating her, one of the children she already had was ill; she might have to go into hospital for a serious operation and several other things too.
>
> I said to her, never mind all that, now just tell me why you really want an abortion. So then she told me it was just too much on top of three children she already had and I thought that quite reasonable and told her so.
>
> But there is no doubt women do feel they have to present a case before a doctor will help.

A survey of doctors' attitudes to abortion showed that 50 per cent are satisfied with the present abortion law, but that 43 per cent would like the law to be more conservative, and it seems probable that this feeling affects the judgements they make when asked for a termination. It is the younger doctors who are the most conservative – doctors under the age of 40 are, in general, more dissatisfied with the abortion law than those over 50.

Thus, the encounters that women have with their GPs and later with the consultants who are asked to do a termination (and who are more inclined to be punitive and unsympathetic in their attitudes than doctors), vary enormously. Suzanna had had a coil fitted and got pregnant using it:

> I have always believed that abortion is available as a back-up to contraception. Well, that seems right to me – if you are making the effort to avoid pregnancy, if you are trusting the methods prescribed and are responsible in using them, then surely abortion ought to be allowed if something goes wrong.
>
> My doctor certainly didn't see it that way. He was amazed the coil had failed but he just wasn't prepared to discuss the idea of abortion. He just said, 'I don't feel able to give my consent. We're talking about social rather than medical reasons aren't we – you're not married are you?' and that was that.

> Grace: My husband is a violent man who has hit me often and it wasn't easy to avoid having sex when he wanted it. I didn't want to get pregnant, not at all, as already I had two small children and I was desperate to leave him, but it just happened. My doctor didn't want to know about all that; he was just disgusted, really disgusted with me and he told me so.

Mandy is a student who had lived with her boyfriend for one and a half years. She got pregnant but her boyfriend did not want the child.

> My GP was very much against me having an abortion. He said he didn't approve and that I was in a steady

relationship and that I was 22 and old enough to have children. I didn't feel anything like old enough. He asked me lots of very intimate questions – it was a bit like having to allow him his fun – then eventually he did agree to help me.

But while, understandably, women remember such encounters with a good deal of distress, those who receive sensitive, supportive treatment from their doctors, are reassured and comforted.

Jenny: My friend made an appointment with the GP because I was in too much of a state to do it. He was kindly, very good really and talked to me for a long time. He suggested all the possibilities and got me to talk them through. But it the end I still felt abortion was the only way and then he was helpful and gave me a letter for the consultant.

Connie: My GP has known me since birth so I didn't much like going to him. It seemed that he would view me quite differently because of what I was asking. But in fact he was incredibly nice and just said 'I don't believe I have the right to tell you what is right or wrong for you.'

Caroline's little boy was just ten months when she found she was pregnant again. Her husband was unemployed and they relied on her work, as a nurse, to bring in money. She says firmly:

'I've never liked the idea of living off the state so this was a big consideration. I went to my GP and he spent a long time with me talking, listening, being very considerate because I kept bursting into tears. He was clearly concerned that this meant I didn't want an abortion, really, and he said that he would support me in any way he could if I went ahead and had the baby. I said I didn't want to bring an unwanted child into the world and he said 'It's not an unwanted child; it's an unwanted pregnancy.' That was the most helpful thing anyone said.

Once a woman's doctor has agreed to recommend her for an NHS abortion, the procedure is that he or she provides one of the two medical practitioners' signatures required before the abortion can be performed. The other generally comes from the consultant, who is the person to decide whether the woman may have a termination.

That some doctors dislike abortion and feel it goes against the reasons they chose to go into medicine is understandable; others have religious beliefs which they feel do not allow them to participate in an abortion. It seems right that there be a conscientious objector's clause which permits these doctors and like-minded nurses to opt out of participating in abortions. Against this is the argument that most people are expected to do unpalatable things at some time, in the name of work, that there is no other area of medicine (even electric-shock therapy) where medical people may refuse to do their job because they do not like it. Even so, it seems better that committed anti-abortionists are not placed in a position of caring for women whose ability to cope with the abortion experience can be very clearly affected by condemnation and criticism, at a time when they are very vulnerable. A woman doctor, writing a personal column in a medical magazine describes the endless talk among consultants about women's morality, and their use of abortion as contraception. She recalls one who came in while she was operating and asked, 'Killing more babies, are we?' Connie has never forgotten the consultant who came to see her when she was in bed, waiting to be called for her operation. He looked at her notes and said, 'I see. Inconvenient for your holiday, is it?'

Although anti-abortionists do not believe the conscientious objectors' clause is strong enough, the Lane Committee investigating the workings of the Abortion Act felt that it

was adequate;[17] and it is interesting that few doctors actually invoke this clause. Rather it appears there are doctors
who enjoy being in the powerful position of arbiter over
women's sexual mores and fertility. Isabel Allen's found
that the majority of GPs spoken to did referrals but decided
what grounds the woman would have an abortion on.[18]
Although there are many tales of gynaecologists being
punitive and hard-line in their attitude to women, most
reported to Isabel Allen that they had 'liberal' policies, and
she concludes: 'There were clearly different interpretations
of the word.' But the very fact that doctors see themselves in
the position of deciding whether to be 'liberal' or not,
suggests a belief in *their* right to choose whether or not a
woman can have an abortion.

It is at this early stage, then, that women tend to
encounter the force not only of views hostile to abortion,
but also the power of the medical establishment to allow
their feelings to be more important than the woman's own
choice. And there is little doubt that the attitude of doctors
and specialists at this early, most difficult stage can have a
profound effect on how the woman goes on to feel about
her abortion and herself.

> Mandy: My doctor's words about immoral students,
> suggesting that we are just a great mass with nothing to
> choose between us because we're all bad, still rankle.
> And at the time because I was feeling very emotional and
> upset they turned me upside down, made me feel
> terribly, terribly sleazy.

> Jill: The consultant suggested I was killing a baby
> because I wanted to go on having a comfortable life. In
> fact we have no money and little space for another child
> and in different circumstances I would have liked
> another. It really hurt; I had felt quite confident that,
> however sadly, I was making the right decision and it

would be understood. Suddenly I saw him as expressing the way the world would judge me. I just wanted to hide myself away feeling everyone would see me as selfish and evil. And that feeling lasted quite a long time.

Fiona: I was only 17 when I got pregnant and even if I had felt able to cope with a child my boyfriend would have been chucked out of the family business. But the doctor didn't see it like that. He looked at me with such disgust and told me I was only getting rid of this child because it was inconvenient.

He told me to have it adopted but I just couldn't have gone through that. I have a friend who did that and she's just so unhappy, she's really gone to pieces and I don't know when she'll ever get over it.

Gemma: The gynaecologist started by 'wondering' whether my pregnancy was by the same man I was living with. Then treating me like a moron, he told me that if I was going to have intercourse of course I would get pregnant. And although I pointed out that the man had been taking what is called precautions, he ignored it. He gave me a really painful examination – like he was punishing me – then he said he would help me out this once. I went out feeling ghastly and indebted to him, which I didn't like.

If a woman chooses to get an abortion on the NHS, she may have to put up with hostility, disapproval or refusal, and although for anyone who feels confident and assertive enough, it is possible to search around for a doctor and consultant who will help, such obstacles can only add to any distress a woman already feels, as well as delaying the abortion itself. This is why slightly more than half the women who have terminations each year have them privately, even though it may well mean considerable financial hardship to do so. Those women who go to the private organizations from the start usually do so because they know they will be seen quickly, that the chances are they will get an early abortion, and that they will not have to put up with criticism or moralizing. For the private abortion organizations exist to support women's right to choose and work from the assumption that she should be the one to work out what is best for her life.

Others go to the private sector after finding that they will not be able to get an NHS abortion or because they cannot cope with the idea of going through with the operation in a place where doctors and nursing staff will regard them as 'bad'. Others go private because the delay in waiting for a hospital bed means they will have to be pregnant for an intolerably long time. Because the abortion clinics are set up specifically to do abortions, they have a system which is fast and efficient. This means that women rarely have to wait more than a few days after their initial appointment and counselling session to have the operation, and most women who use the clinics (especially those operated by BPAS and PAS) regard them as making abortion as little distressing as possible.

Anne, who had 'fallen pregnant' by a now absent boyfriend went to her GP who was highly critical.

> He went on at me about how silly I had been and how people who took care didn't get pregnant. In the end he said he would give me a letter of recommendation but he had no idea how long it would take for me to get an appointment.
>
> I didn't have the money to go private but in the end I borrowed it from a friend, in desperation, because I couldn't face a long wait. And what a contrast when I went to the private place. They were really nice and made me feel I was unlucky rather than stupid. It was just such a relief being there after my GP.

Those who were not so happy with the private clinics (the number of interviewees for this book who felt that way were very few) disliked the realization that they are just one of many other women in the same position. One woman described it as like being on a conveyor belt. Clearly the feeling of being an individual who is in some way special and whose situation and emotions are deserving of particular concern, takes a knock.

> Liz: I suppose I had seen myself as rather a dramatic, tragic figure. I felt at least that my suffering was something out of the ordinary. Going to a place where there were so many women all in the same position, whose stories were probably just as bad as mine, made me feel rather miserable. I think I felt let down.

> Rhona: It just didn't feel very nice, all those women sitting there like cattle waiting to get their abortions organized. No, I didn't like that. I would have liked a bit more privacy.

There is a good deal of criticism of private clinics from the anti-abortion lobby which maintains that they are in 'business' and so 'urge' women to have abortions. This may be true of some private profit-making clinics, and pro-choice people working in the field warn that it is wise to make some enquiries about the clinic you consider going to – you could, for example, ring up one of the charity bodies. But the criticism is certainly not true of BPAS and PAS which are registered charities and therefore do not profit from 'productivity'. It is a view which Margery, counsellor with one of the large charities, responds to angrily:

> We gain absolutely nothing by encouraging women to have abortions, but that is the kind of thinking which can so easily be believed. Once you start painting a picture of abortion as a way people get rich quick, of

course it all looks very undesirable. That was a lot truer in the days of illegal abortion.

It's a red herring, a way of discrediting the idea of abortion and getting the law repealed. I would be perfectly happy to be put out of business if the need for abortion would disappear because a really safe, reliable contraceptive was developed, but that is not happening. Nor are the anti-abortionists doing any campaigning in that direction.

Meanwhile women do get pregnant when they do not want to; there are still and probably will always be girls and women who get in a muddle with contraceptives or who have unprotected sex. There are women who are forced to have sex and I don't just mean rape by a stranger – I mean within marriage. There are girls subjected to incest who get pregnant and there must be an abortion back-up service for them.

What the anti-abortion lobby seems not to realize is that none of us enjoys the idea of abortion, but we do see that it is necessary and we are trying to provide a humane and caring way of coping with that situation. To be humane and caring is not the same as urging people or encouraging them and that needs saying too.

It is, then, at the point when she must make a decision about abortion and set about organizing it, that a woman faces the minefield of morality, emotion and control which exist around the matter. Abortion brings most powerfully into focus the belief of our medical profession that it has the right to make fundamental and intimate decisions about women's fertility. While women are expected to take most major decisions about welfare, health and conduct, an unplanned pregnancy means that they must go cap in hand to beg for help and make sure the 'reasons' are good enough.

The issue is, of course, complicated by the fact that we do

acknowledge that doctors have a greater knowledge of health than the lay person and that their knowledge about what is best for our physical welfare may be greater than our own. But whereas in most areas of health we, as patients, may make choices about whether or not we will undergo operations or take treatment, in the matter of abortion this power of choice often does not exist.

6. The Abortion

I think they took me for the operation at about a quarter
to ten and I remember looking at the clock and I was
back in the ward and it was all over and I just wanted to
cry and cry. (Meg)

I had my few things packed and I just kept watching the
clock until it was time to go. I went by train and settled
myself down and began to think about why I was there.
Tears began to roll down my cheeks as I thought how
different it might have been under other circumstances.
As I got to the dreaded place I saw about 20 other girls
sat around. I joined them and then we were asked for
money. Great, I thought, first things first. Then it was
down to business: blood tests, wrist bands, queuing to
see the doctor and then there was a wait until we had to
go in. (Anne)

I was in a ward with women trying to have babies, and I
was told not to say a word about why I was there. It made
me feel awful, like a leper or something and the staff
treated me as a nuisance, someone using up a bed
unnecessarily. (Dina)

I felt quite in control when I went into the hospital. I felt
very sure I was making the right decision and that
nobody had the right to criticize me. The staff were
neutral towards me – they weren't particularly friendly,
but they were efficient and I didn't want more. I was just
very relieved when it was all over.

Women talking about their feelings on the day of the abortion demonstrate vividly how personal and intimate an experience it is. While the details may have been similar, the way the women expressed them was not. Some women recalled the actual event from the time they entered a hospital or clinic to the time of departure with anguish, a sense of fear and of being disapproved of, while others were surprised and relieved to find that the day itself was less harrowing than the time leading up to it.

Although the operation is the focal point of the experience, the way it is perceived and felt is coloured by events leading up to it. The attitude of doctors to women when they request termination is highly significant, but the length of time they must wait before having the operation is likely to be just as significant and in many cases even more so. A woman's body becomes daily more adapted to pregnancy, and in many cases less willing to 'free' her from nature's push to make her maternal. In some cases the unpleasant symptoms end quickly and the woman begins to feel good, to experience a relationship with the growing foetus; others battle to suppress such feelings. Not surprisingly, much of the research done into the aftermath of abortion suggests that a delay in waiting for abortion adds considerably to the trauma.

It is a point which Linda Clarke makes: 'Any delay in obtaining an abortion, at whatever stage of gestation the operation is performed, contributes to the stress and anxiety experienced by women'.[19] Professor Peter Huntingford argues: 'Obviously women suffer if they must wait and it takes an inhumane system to add this to the feelings they anyway may have about choosing abortion. It would not be difficult to set up a far more humane way if the medical profession were committed to it.'

The Royal College of Obstetricians and Gynaecologists, carrying out an extensive study into the reasons for late abortions found that in 1981, 16 per cent of all abortions were carried out in the second trimester (after 12 weeks) which they considered a matter for concern. The document reporting the research states: 'A legal abortion carried out in the mid trimester is often associated with less social and moral acceptability [than an early abortion], greater psychological cost and an increased risk of complications, morbidity and mortality.'[20]

So what causes the delays? Why is it that one woman who approaches her doctor within a month of a missed period gets her termination at nine weeks, while another must wait until eleven weeks or even later?

One frequent cause of delay is the time it takes for a pregnancy test to be done on the NHS. A woman who goes to one of the pregnancy advisory bureaux or a chemist or who does her own home test gets a result on the same or at least the next day. Those who go to a GP's practice, however, where samples are sent or taken to a hospital, must often wait a week or more for the result before they can even begin to discuss the situation with their doctor. It has been suggested that some GPs who disapprove of abortion may deliberately delay pregnancy test results. Isabel Allen found that 'Delay in general was attributed to professionals rather than patients, which again confirms what women suspected. There was certainly evidence of delay caused by the mechanics of referral and a lack of any sense of urgency on the part of GPs who often used second-class post or did not telephone consultants, some of whom were very keen on GPs discussing cases with them on the telephone.'[21]

On the other hand, women tend to be blamed by doctors for delay. The Royal College of Obstetricians and Gynaecologists (RCOG) noted: 'Reasons given by doctors included denial of pregnancy by women, apprehension, indecision, financial difficulty and the disruption of a relationship.'[22] This has not been the finding of other research. Linda Clarke found that three-quarters of the women wanting abortion had seen a doctor by eight weeks,[23] while Dr John Ashton, surveying a group of women in Wessex, found that almost half reported pregnancy within seven weeks.[24]

Linda, a mother of a young child who found herself pregnant again within a year of giving birth, remembers:

> I went to my doctor very quickly because I was quite sure I didn't want another baby then. My doctor didn't like it, you could tell, but very grudgingly he said he would get me a pregnancy test 'to make sure'. So I took my urine sample in next day but then it took eleven days before I got the result back and he said he wasn't prepared to discuss my request for a referral until then.

The RCOG also made the point that one factor which is not mentioned by doctors, but which they know to be a cause of delay, is fear of the doctor's reaction – an observation borne out by research done for this book as well as those working in private bureaux who frequently see young women at a late stage of pregnancy, who explain that they have not dared to approach 'our doctor'. Cheryl, 18, was pregnant by a recent boyfriend. She was terrified at the idea of going to the GP who has been her doctor since childhood: 'I was just too scared of what he would say to me and of him telling my mum. I wanted to just get what had to be done over without a fuss. But it took a lot of courage to go to my doctor.' Louise said: 'I was that scared of going to my GP. He's a really upright, elderly man and I knew he would think me awful. And I was right – he called me promiscuous (which I'm not) and lectured me for ten minutes. Then he said if he helped me, he didn't ever want to see me in this state again.' Melanie had already heard of the reputation of the GP at the college where she was studying: 'I dreaded going because she was known to be very hard on students. And that was true. She took the line that she would help because it was clearly stupid to throw away my education, but she also gave me a hell of a lecture. Not a word about my boyfriend, mind, except to say, "It takes two to tango." '

Understandably, it is the young who generally fear disapproval and their doctors 'lecturing' most. And it is the young who are likely to be latest in seeking help when they find they are pregnant. As well as fearing medical disapproval, these girls may also pretend to themselves that the pregnancy is not real; they ignore the symptoms, hoping the problem will go away. Teenagers account for more than 40 per cent of abortions after 12 weeks and more than 50 per cent after 20 weeks. Caroline Bailey of Brook Advisory Centres, where they see a high percentage of young women, comments on this: 'I am sure the young do try to hide the fact of conception and pregnancy from themselves as well as others. They cannot face the implications of knowing so they will not seek help until they think they look pregnant and this may be very late on. A girl who doesn't show much will go on telling herself the symptoms are "in the mind" or indigestion!'

But while the young have a tendency to delude themselves, research has also demonstrated that it is this group which is most likely to be delayed or refused abortion when they do go for help. Tracey, 16, went to the doctor on her own first and remembers:

> He said he just didn't agree with abortion, he wasn't able to help. He was really unhelpful and didn't take any notice of my tears, and I was that panicky because I was only a kid myself and I couldn't see coping with this. So I went home and told me mum and she phoned the doctor and made another appointment and we went together. She just told him I ought to have an abortion and he took notice of her.

Ruth, 18, had never slept with a boy before she met Darren. She thought he was 'in love' with her and when she found she was pregnant, she told him with much delight.

> He just looked at me and said, 'It can't be mine.' Like

that. I couldn't believe my ears. I had never been with anyone else. Then he said he had been meaning to tell me our affair was over. He didn't love me any more. So I was left and I didn't know what on earth to do. It was that awful. Luckily I had one close friend and I told her and she knew that you have to go to your doctor. So I went to this doctor I'd never seen before in our practice and he was kind of smarmy to me and said he would do what he could. But then he said I must come back for another appointment because he wanted to consider the situation before he decided whether he could help me with an abortion or not.

It is not only GPs who cause delay. Even when a woman has been referred to a gynaecologist things do not necessarily go smoothly. Consultants do not, by any means, always grant a termination because a GP recommends it. If her request is refused, the woman must start 'shopping around' for an abortion, which causes a considerable delay. The delay is lessened if she can immediately afford to go privately – and plenty of women do so at this stage – but if she cannot afford this choice, there is a very real risk of her pregnancy going over three months.

It is a situation which concerned consultant obstetricians based in Newcastle, Mr John Lawson and Mr Leonard Barren, have seen and which led to their setting up a highly efficient patient-centred service. They started by finding out the number of abortions done annually in their catchment area, from which it was possible to predict what would be required in further years (the figures remain fairly constant on Tyneside as they do nationally). They then enlisted all consultants in the area willing to do abortions and set up a central appointments system. Mr Lawson explains:

This was a vital part of getting an efficient scheme. So often a doctor rings the consultant he knows to be sympathetic to abortion and finds he has a long list, which of course means a delay. We have a special telephone number for the service which a GP can ring and find out which of the consultants can do his termination first.

This has cut delays enormously and has substantially reduced the number of late abortions done in our area. That means economies to the health service and, significantly, it means a great deal less distress for the patient. It also means that the patient has a reasonable period of time to consider her decision if she wishes, whereas a woman who knows her pregnancy is going into second trimester will feel a great deal more pressurized.

But obviously the essence of this service is that we are a group of doctors who feel that abortion must be available to women and although we have occasions when we do not grant terminations because we feel there is too much ambivalence in the woman's mind, we are very willing to consider her right to decide what is best.

The clearest demonstration of this scheme's success is that 90 per cent of abortions done in Newcastle are performed on the NHS and this is a fine example of the way a humane, patient-centred system can be organized. Similarly the day-care clinics around the country provide a service which is geared to the needs and wishes of the patient.

Connie had an abortion at a London day-care clinic after being refused termination by the consultant she saw at a large teaching hospital. Looking back, she is pleased that her sympathetic GP acted swiftly and referred her to the consultant in charge of the day-care clinic.

It had just opened at King's College Hospital. I remember having an outpatient's appointment and the man saying, 'Why do you want a termination?' I was very defensive because I'd had such a bad time with the consultant before, but he wasn't trying to change my mind, just giving me a chance to talk.

I went along on the day and there were about six of us going in at the same time. I had a chat with the sister who was incredibly sympathetic and nice and when it was my turn to go along she held my hand. She did that all the way through. They were doing the operations without general anaesthetic and the doctor warned me when he had to inject my cervix. It did hurt but only briefly, then they inserted the suction device and it was all over.

It wasn't frightening because there wasn't a big wait. I was able to go in, have it done and then go. There was no big ordeal and it was wonderful being among people who were so kind.

The supportiveness, the sense of people being 'on your side' is the thing which people going to reputable private clinics talk of most. Clearly this is all-important and is where the greatest contrast lies between some abortions on the NHS and those in private clinics. Those dealing with patients stress the importance of giving women appropriate information when they face an abortion. Caroline Bailey points out that this does not necessarily mean telling all.

I believe that a woman should feel she knows what to expect, broadly, but I think some women want and can cope with more detailed information than others. If a girl is obviously feeling very bad about the implications of a termination, I would not be keen to give her a graphic description of what goes on. But others do want that and then they are entitled to be told.

Equally, if a girl is going in for a late abortion which involves actually delivering the foetus, I think it is important she knows what to expect.

In research carried out by Isabel Allen, it was found that many women did not feel they had been adequately informed, particularly in NHS abortions.[25] Allen found a huge discrepancy between the availability of material for women in the public and private sector. Only 11 per cent of women in the NHS had been given any written information compared with 72 per cent of private patients. When it came to spoken information, more than three-quarters of private patients had been given information, compared with 50 per cent in the NHS.

The kind of information women most want – primarily the risks attached to abortion – is often presented in its worst light by those who disapprove of the choice. Antonia Hopkins at SPUC talks of the dangers of infertility and infection women face with abortion and similar ideas are put about by doctors dealing with patients. As Julia South writes, 'It is put about that women who have abortions may become sterile, or may have great problems conceiving or bringing a baby to term. This is the price to be paid, is what is implied; and many believe it.'[26] A study by the RCOG of 7,000 women who had abortions between 1976 and 1979 provides useful data.[27] This report found *no* significant increase in the incidence of miscarriage, ectopic pregnancy, stillbirth, prematurity or low-birth-weight babies amongst women who had abortions and who later went on to have a child. (However, it is thought that multiple abortions can lead to problems, particularly miscarriage.)

Interestingly, while so much ethical opposition exists to abortion, remarkably little is said about the ending of women's fertility at the time of abortion. Statistics demonstrate a large difference in the number of sterilizations done at the time of abortion on the NHS and in the private sector – with the NHS having the higher number. Of course this figure may be affected by the fact that a woman going privately will have to pay for her sterilization and may not be able to afford to do so, even if she wishes, at the same time as paying for termination. But Professor Huntingford is convinced that there are occasions when women are 'persuaded' to have a sterilization with their abortions – a practice which has been found to increase the risk of physical complications.

Hall and Illsley[28] make the point that it is bad practice to even offer sterilization at the same time as abortion because 'The woman may – rightly or wrongly – perceive the offer of abortion as being linked to her acceptance of sterilization'. They also have grave doubts about whether women should be expected to consider something as irreversible as sterilization when undergoing the stress of an abortion.

For all that, it is clear that a 'package deal' is often made. In a case reported in the *Sunday Mirror* (30 September 1984) a woman who was told by her doctor that she could not have an NHS abortion unless she agreed to sterilization, received damages from the local health authority.

> Mary: I was sent by my GP to a consultant who twice refused to give me a termination. He interrogated me for more than an hour on why I wouldn't have the baby. Then when he did eventually agree, he told me I would have to be sterilized at the same time. I didn't want this as I really hoped to have a baby at another time, when my circumstances would be better. But he went on delaying until I agreed, and then the abortion was done at four and a half months.
>
> So since then I have never been able to have a child and I have lived with terrible regret and sadness. It was blackmail and I really believed before this that the medical profession are there to relieve suffering, not to cause it.
>
> Rose: I was 42 when I went into hospital for my termination and I was waiting in bed for the operation when the consultant who I hadn't met before came around the ward. First he started making difficulties – I think he took a dislike to me because I was quite confident. In a sneery tone, he asked me questions in

front of his juniors and started saying he hadn't had a signed letter from my doctor and wasn't sure if he was going to do the operation. Then finally he said, 'So do you want to be sterilized?' I didn't, not in the least, but equally I was sure I didn't want children and I reckoned he wouldn't give me an abortion if I didn't agree, so I said yes.

Clearly these sorts of incidents can profoundly affect the way a woman will feel about her abortion, but the actual time when the operation is performed is discussed in even more emotional terms.

Some women commented on how strange it felt to realize that the day had come, that the turmoil, the agonizing, the talk of the days or weeks before had led inexorably to the time of the operation. Others simply felt relief at knowing that the waiting was over. For some the day is recalled as a complete blank, hazy or surreal. Others remember details and feelings vividly.

Lorna: Actually getting myself through the door, into the clinic was the hardest thing. I knew that this was it and I had a strong feeling that life was never going to be the same again. Then I just cut off my feelings and they told me to get undressed, which bed to use, and I just existed like that until they wheeled me off to the theatre.

7. Illegal Abortion

The two anti-abortion organizations, SPUC and LIFE, were created after the passing of the 1967 Abortion Act. Their aim was to mount organized campaigns to protest at what they view as a law which legitimizes child murder and to gain support for their view that the rights of the 'innocent' foetus are paramount.

This flurry of activity gave the impression that before the passing of the Act abortion was not an issue which required attention and confrontation; it was as though abortion came into being because a law was passed permitting it in certain circumstances. But of course this is a wrong impression. Women have paid others to abort them or have performed abortions on themselves for as long as the history of fertility is charted. The Abortion Act, recognizing this, was passed to try to prevent some of the damage done by illegal abortions.

In the twelfth century in Britain, a sufficient number of abortions were being procured for it to be made an offence under canon law; by the thirteenth century it had become illegal under common law. In the Offences Against the Person Act of 1861 it became a criminal offence for a woman to 'administer to herself poison or any other noxious thing' or to 'use an instrument or other means' with the intention of procuring a miscarriage. Nevertheless, the need for abortions was pressing enough that women submitted themselves to methods which varied from instruments, sticks or knitting needles being inserted into the uterus to dislodge the foetus, to substances being inserted through the vagina.

Peggy Wakelin, a pregnancy counsellor, recalls a young girl coming to see her shortly after the Abortion Act had been passed, who had burnt herself badly with caustic soda, in an attempt to miscarry. Herbal remedies were popular and while some may have been ineffective and harmless, others were ineffective and poisonous. Some certainly did cause miscarriage but this was because they poisoned the woman and caused such internal disruption that the foetus was displaced. Germaine Greer,[29] describing some of the substances used – black hellebore, oil of juniper, seneca snakeroot, oils of pennyroyal, rue and parsley – explains:

> Mistaking the dose of purgatives and poisons can lead to uncontrollable results – drastic uterine damage and death. Most herbal abortifacients, if taken by mouth, exert a double action, on the one hand, simply toxic and on the other, uterine stimulant. The woman makes herself so sick that the life of the foetus is jeopardized and the direct action of the drug on the uterine muscle expels the dead or dying foetus.

So women, in their desperation, took the very real risk of injury or death rather than give birth to a child they felt they could not take into their lives. Dr R.F. Gardner, in his thoughtful analysis of a Christian response to abortion,[30] also points out that women have risked prosecution to perform abortions out of compassion and concern for their own sex. He points to research done in 1966 which showed that over 80 per cent of convicted abortionists were women, and he paints a vivid picture of the way in which things worked. The women

> mostly became involved by first succeeding in aborting themselves by use of an enema syringe and, then, as word got round, being begged to help relatives and later friends. Eventually pressures built up, the threat of suicide if they wouldn't help. There was no doubt that compassion and feminine solidarity were strongly motivating factors among the women who had acquired this skill.

They could share the feelings of the suppliant in her plight, or imagine how they would feel if it were their own teenage daughter or granddaughter who was 'in trouble'. Financial reward played little part in their activities. They were proud that they had saved marriages and homes.

But it is also true that a substantial number of those performing 'back-street' abortions in the days before the Abortion Act were men, some qualified doctors using their skills illegally out of a genuine belief in the rightness of abortion, others finding it a highly profitable form of private practice. Others were untrained and it is easy to see how the illicit situation allowed charlatans to flourish. It is also known that the risk of death or injury through illegal abortion was substantial. As recently as the 1930s, Dr John Ashton records: 'the known number of deaths related to abortion in England and Wales was running at more than 450 per annum'. Since the Abortion Act was passed, there have been only a tiny number of deaths. In countries where abortion remains illegal, deaths connected with the operation continue to be high.

Whatever the risks of abortion, women have always been prepared to take them when the urgency of their situation required it. When abortion was not possible, women have resorted to infanticide, and in some cultures this continues to be a solution. A National Opinion Poll carried out in the UK in 1966 found that 4 per cent of women admitted that they had had an induced abortion and 11 per cent said they had attempted to induce one themselves. In the view of Irma Kurtz, 'agony aunt' for *Cosmopolitan*, 'When circumstances make it intolerable for a woman to have a child, she will get an abortion. Whether she tries to do it herself or resorts to the back-street quack, she will find a way. Women will not be forced to have babies they cannot care for and do not want.'

Why is it that anti-abortionists are not so active or voci-ferous in their objection to terminations carried out illeg-ally, which inflict far greater harm to the foetus, as well as the mother, than do legal terminations? Is the sanctity of the life of the foetus less urgent under these conditions? The answer, apparently, is that it is the law which is wrong rather than the practice. The anti-abortionists are commit-ted to having the law repealed because, in the words of Antonia Hopkins at SPUC, 'It is essentially a bad law which has permitted the taking of human lives. It has not improved conditions or benefitted women.'

The point she makes is that the need for abortion should be tackled by making conditions better for women who are pregnant, so that they can go ahead and have the child. In cases where this is what the woman wants few of us would disagree, including active members of the pro-choice lobby like Joanna Chambers of the Birth Control Trust who says:

> None of us likes abortion; I certainly wish it did not have to exist. But there is little effort going into devising such effective forms of birth control that it will be eliminated. Until this happens and until life is made a great deal easier for women with children, abortion seems to me an absolutely essential right.

But SPUC and other anti-abortionists are not conspicu-ous for the pressure they put on the government to improve the lot of women and children. LIFE, it is true, runs a hous-ing scheme to help pregnant women who want to go ahead and have their babies, and this is clearly a valuable step, but it is far from being enough to persuade women who seek an abortion that having a child is preferable.

In fact, the anti-abortionists seem to have a mystical belief that if the Abortion Act would go away, everything would be all right. Yet doctors who have coped with the results of women's attempts to get abortions they could not have legally know very well how much more damage is done under these circumstances. Maggie, an articulate, loving mother of two grown children, makes plain, with her description of an illegal abortion, just how terrible the experience is and what women will endure in order to get free of a pregnancy they cannot tolerate. Listening to her painful memories the question is begged, is this what the anti-abortionists really want?

I remember so clearly seeing for the first time the man who was going to do my abortion. He was like all the worst ideas you have about back-street abortionists. I got his number from a girlfriend and when I phoned him he was very very cautious and wanted to know how I had got his number. After we had talked he agreed to come to the flat of a friend, but he told me I must only have one other person with me. I felt terribly frightened. I thought the next thing I'd know would be the police at the door.

When he came to do the abortion, he told me to undress and I had to get on the bed. He used a syringe to squirt something into me. I suspect it was soapy water – I later learned that that is what was often used. I paid him £150 and he was going to go.

Then the pain began and it was frightful, just terrible. I jack-knifed and screamed in pain and the girl who was with me came rushing in. He shouted, 'Get out – get out.' Then it calmed down a bit and I remember we waited, drinking endless cups of coffee and eventually there was a small show of blood and I thought right, that's it.

It wasn't until eight days later that I realized I was still pregnant. I hadn't had a period and I still had the symptoms and sure enough when I went for the test it was positive. I remember having to pretend to be delighted and feeling petrified and wondering what on earth to do.

I was 24 at the time and the man I had been having an

affair with, and thought was going to live with me, had returned to his wife and I was absolutely alone, trying to earn my living. My mother was widowed and she wouldn't have been able to help, so I knew I had to get rid of it somehow.

In desperation I went to my family GP who was a dear man but he couldn't help me, although he did say he wouldn't tell my mother and he wouldn't stand in my way of sorting it out. I appreciated that.

So I phoned up the abortionist – he was a psychiatric nurse – again and said I was still pregnant and he was very angry with me and asked for more money. I said no, I paid you to do a job and you haven't done it, so come and finish things. At first he refused but then I pointed out he was in a very vulnerable position, so he did come again to the flat.

But this time he insisted on touching me up, as 'payment' before he would help. It was appalling, repulsive – but I felt I had no choice but to let him.

He syringed me again and went away saying, 'This time it will work for sure.' This time it wasn't so painful, rather like period cramps – that was all. So I lay all day on a plastic sheet I had bought, waiting for something to happen. But by the evening when my friend came in nothing had happened. I just felt panic-stricken and dreadful.

It turned out that the man she was going out with was a gynaecologist and he was very kind and agreed to help, although of course he had to be very very careful. He said the foetus would almost certainly be damaged after all I'd been through and might well be dead. He said there were no drugs available which would finish the abortion and he suggested using a full bottle of fizzy drink inserted into my vagina. He explained that the gases would act. And I remember him saying, 'This won't be very nice for you because you will go into labour.'

And I did. I was in labour for about 12 hours and I was all on my own when, suddenly, there was lots of blood and water and a thud and there between my legs was a baby. It looked like a little rubber doll.

I held it in my hands and I cried and cried. I knelt on the floor with this tiny baby in my hand and cried until I couldn't cry any more. Then I wrapped him in cotton wool and then newspaper and then I took him into the bathroom and laid him on the back of the lavatory so that the gynaecologist could take him away. But I wished afterwards that I had buried him.

The experience of an illegal abortion, before 1967, turned writer Anna Raeburn into a committed campaigner for legal abortion for all women who decide they want one. Writing in a women's magazine, she recalled:

Friends asked me to contact a man called Martin who claimed to be a doctor – at least his hands and his instruments were scrupulously clean. Before he came, we covered the bed in my room in a bleak North London flat, with newspapers and polythene.

Martin used a syringe-type douche filled with soap and water and quinine. When he put the liquid into my womb, the pain hit my stomach like a pointed lead weight. I was sick. He gave me pain killers. I gave him £40. He left. I bled for six weeks and wound up in hospital with a doctor telling me that such a practice could have left me sterile. Or killed me.

Many people, including those who disapprove of 'the liberal' way the Abortion Act is often interpreted feel relief that the back-street abortionist no longer exists. Yet SPUC maintain that illegal abortion is still carried out and they point to their research which claims 1,336 illegal abortions in 1978 and use this as a further argument to demonstrate that the Abortion Act has not improved the situation.

What is more plausible is that illegal abortions are still performed because legal ones are either too difficult or take too long to arrange. The Lane Committee, reporting on the functioning of the Act in the early 1970s, found cases of girls and women attempting to induce their own abortions because they had been refused doctors' consent. They cited the case of a 16-year-old girl:

> When she found she was pregnant, she decided to try and get an abortion; 'I went to the doctor but he told me that no-one around here would say I was suitable for abortion. He told me to have it in a home and get it adopted. I am adopted and no child of mine is going to be, if I can help it.'
>
> After this, she decided on self-abortion. 'I knew I couldn't get myself enough money to pay for one, so I decided I would have to get rid of it myself. My friend got me some pills and I knocked myself around a lot and generally did everything I wasn't supposed to. I couldn't face using a knitting needle as my friend did after being told she couldn't have an abortion either. Anyway I had a miscarriage.'

It is clear that women's health and sanity is vastly more at risk when they must resort to illegal practices than when abortion is legalized. Even if sanctity of life were the central issue, it is difficult to believe that returning to a situation where back-street abortions are common rather than exceptional is the best way to help the foetus.

8. After the Abortion

At the time I thought I would never get over it. I felt a tremendous sense of loss and I think I was quite crazy for a while. I felt like pushing women with babies under trains and I couldn't go to see a friend who had had a baby for weeks. (Lisa)

The worst part of the abortion for me was the after-effects, mentally. There was no-one I could talk to, my GP told me to pull myself together, my boyfriend was too upset and even now doesn't really like to talk about it and I didn't know of any after-abortion counselling in my area. I doubt my feelings about it will ever get better – for me it was a traumatic experience; one that I would never wish to repeat. (Tracey)

For the operation I took a day off work and next day I was back in the office. I was weak for a while but physically and mentally I felt great and I haven't thought about it much since. (Diana)

I don't feel bad about the abortion. I feel bad about me. If I hadn't put myself in the position of having sex when I didn't even want it, I wouldn't have had to have an abortion. So I'm angry with myself. (Shirley)

Once the abortion is over, women must cope with the experience, assimilate it, learn to live with what has been done. It is a very different situation from dealing with the time before the abortion which may well be painful, confused and frightening but which is, at least, a finite period leading up to an event.

The time after has no such shape and form. The event is history and the future is not marked with a moment when distress, despair, self-dislike – all frequent and understandable reactions to abortion – will end. Nor is there a set pattern of feelings, behaviour and emotions which can be predicted for women after their operations. Women react very differently to what counsellor Caroline Bailey describes as 'a very real life crisis – the one death you know in advance is going to happen'.

Some women find – often to their surprise – that they do not feel bad after the abortion. There is a sense of enormous relief that the event is passed. Some suffer and 'go through' their feelings so thoroughly before the termination that the operation is the end, the tying up of their emotional drama. Women who have been clear from the start that for them abortion is morally and practically a correct choice, may well assimilate the experience with little if any pain.

> Jeanette: I had talked and talked about the abortion before I went for the operation. I found out as much as I could about what the experience would be like, from the look of the clinic, to the kind of anaesthetic they used, to what the operation entails. I had gone over and over the options – what having a child would mean, and I felt very very clear that I knew what I was doing.
>
> So when I came out from the clinic I felt as though I was free. I was free of having to think further and I felt sure I hadn't made a mistake. It wasn't something I took lightly – I did a lot of heart searching, there was a good deal of pain before but by the time it was done I think I had been through anything which would have caused pain.

> Lisa: I'll never forget the abortion and in a way I think it's important that I shouldn't; it's not something to be dismissed as nothing. But just the same I have no regrets

at all. Sometimes I worry about that, perhaps I should feel some guilt or something, but I don't and I'm so grateful I had the opportunity to get an abortion and that my mum stood by me.

Jackie: As I had never wanted children and I got pregnant because of a contraceptive failure, I had no guilt about choosing abortion. I do believe that we, women, have the right to decide about this – there really isn't anyone else who is in the position to decide, is there? So when I got pregnant and I knew I didn't want a child, there wasn't a dilemma. But I didn't risk the disapproval of doctors because I know I might have got upset, and I didn't see why they should be allowed to upset me. No, luckily I could afford to go privately.

For many women the time following an abortion is not so simple, so painless. Many do experience relief that the event which has involved so much thought, conflict and personal upheaval is over. But that relief may well be interwoven with a profound sense of loss and guilt at the irrevocability of what has been done. One woman described poignantly a common feeling when she said:

I realized once it was over that I didn't like myself for what I had done. I still felt it was the right – well really the only – thing that could have been done but I felt flawed; I had this strong sense when I went out that people could see what I had done and that they would be judging me as bad.

Some women who have assumed that life will be as it was before they got pregnant are shocked to find that it seems dramatically different. Thus Wendy says:

I had in my mind a picture of the happy family life we had with our two kids and I just somehow felt that the pregnancy and the abortion were a separate piece of life, almost a separate life which I had to get through, but then everything would be magically back as it was.

But it wasn't like that. I coped pretty well in the time before the abortion and my husband thought I was really okay about what I was doing. But afterwards, when I came round from the operation, I was crying and it just went on and on for days. I felt I had no right to just be happy; I felt I had failed by getting pregnant and not wanting it and that I had to be punished for that.

I spent most of the first week or two back from the hospital in my room; my husband had to tell the kids I was ill. I felt it wasn't fair on them but I really couldn't pull myself together.

Over and over again, women talk of the isolation and loneliness they feel after an abortion, believing their reaction to be unique and even pathological. In interview after interview the thoughts of Anne were repeated: 'I didn't know it would be so difficult to come to terms with what I have done. I feel I'm the only woman in the world who has done something which seemed necessary, and who feels in pieces about it afterwards.' Particularly daunting and frightening is the feeling many have that their sorrow and grief will be endless. They can see no reason why it should diminish or go away. Yet around them, very often, others – including often a partner – assume the ordeal is over and done with.

Mary: My boyfriend collected me from the clinic and was really kind and caring, and he talked to me a lot for about three days, but then he assumed that was it. That was a reasonable period of rehabilitation. I don't think he was being unkind, he just felt the event was over. But for me it wasn't. I couldn't stop thinking about it and feeling really sad and I just wondered if it would ever go away.

Fiona: I thought it was all over in the recovery room but I couldn't have been more wrong. I *never* stop thinking about my baby and I often feel something is missing – a part of me. This may sound silly but Rob and I still cry together because we always have that unanswered question, 'Did we do the right thing?'

Doubt, wondering whether it was the right decision, is a feeling a good many women have and if they are distressed and angry with themselves, it is understandable that this should be the central question. But in the view of Helena, counsellor at an abortion clinic, people rarely make the wrong decision. She explains:

It is not a bit surprising that women ask themselves this after the abortion. They cannot go back, the chance of the baby is gone and they feel bad. Of course this is the most natural thing to wonder and when you feel distressed none of the reasons which make you decide to have an abortion seem so valid.

But that does not mean it was the wrong choice. The fact is, abortion is not a happy choice; it may be the better of two choices in certain circumstances but if a woman is choosing it because of negative things – no support, no home, no money, no partner – and in other circumstances would have wanted the child, of course she is going to feel unhappy about it.

When counselling women I always talk to them about this, about the fact that an abortion will be part of their history and if I feel they really could not cope with that I would try to help them find a way out other than abortion.

Women experience different levels of distress and for different lengths of time, but a good deal of research done into the psychological after-effects of abortion show that most women suffer for a while but that after a few months they generally improve. The exceptions to this tend to be women with psychiatric problems in the past; cases in which the woman has been bullied into an abortion; or where the abortion has been accompanied by another distressing experience, such as a relationship breaking up at the same time. Psychologist Annabel Broome, discussing the need for women to be supported around the time of abortion, comments:

> The literature . . . does give us enough indication to see that few women suffer severe long-term psychological distress as a result of TOP (termination of pregnancy). In general, women feel reduced anxiety and depression a while after the operation, though a certain level of distress immediately after the operation is very common.[31]

A similar finding was made by Dr John Ashton who looked at the feelings of 64 women after eight weeks and 86 women after eight months.[32] He found that about half the patients were affected by short-lived disturbances including guilt and regrets and sensitivity to the comments of people around them. More than one-third of the group experienced no distressing feelings, while about 5 per cent had enduring, severe psychiatric disturbance. Dr Ashton's research demonstrates that certain factors have a great deal to do with how a woman will feel after her abortion. He says: 'The factors determining a satisfactory outcome seem to be those conducive to a woman making a decision which she believes to be her own in a context where she is accorded respect and support. The development of severe guilt depends not only on the constitution of the woman but on the prevailing social attitudes to her action in under-going an abortion.'

A group of researchers at the Department of Psychological Medicine at University College Hospital in London wrote:

In our view [psychiatric damage] can nearly always be avoided by selection and psychiatric support during the woman's stay in hospital and afterwards. The attitude of those around her is extremely important – and, if adverse, can outweight the psychiatric help provided. The patient's temporary guilt and depression may be deepened by criticisms – spoken or implied – from gynaecologist or nurse.[33]

Yet, as has been seen in earlier chapters, even today, almost 20 years after the Abortion Act, women are sometimes subjected to hostile and vicious treatment by the medical profession and there is little doubt that it has, indeed, caused anguish during and after the event. One single mother in her thirties was told by her consultant: 'It is known of course that women who seek abortions are promiscuous and as a profession we are only encouraged to help them because the fate of a child born to such a woman would be intolerable.' The effect of this, she recalls, was

like something burning into my head. I had felt quite all right up until then – not happy about what I was having to do, but it seemed the best as I just couldn't have managed two kids on my own. But after that I felt horrible. And when I came out of hospital I felt like muck, truly disgusting and the feeling went on and on making me very miserable.

It was recognition of just this, of the fact that after the operation women have to live at ease with themselves, which made the doctor who works in an abortion day-care clinic, write of the way she now works:

In the day-care clinic all the staff see abortion as a woman's right. Our role is to provide an atmosphere where women can make the right choice for themselves, with all the medical information, counselling and support that they need. And we support each other so that any problems are resolved between us rather than being turned against the women.

The years of doing this work have given me a certain ability to notice ambivalence, and to pick out those (very few) women who come to the abortion service but who do not actually want an abortion. It often takes far more time and energy to give a woman the opportunity to realize that she really wants a child and that she can cope. And I see that as an equally important part of my job, although more difficult and more time-consuming. It is vital that the risks and possible long-term complications of abortion are fully explained so that women can make informed decisions.

It is still the case that most women having, or attempting to obtain, abortions in this country get little support when undergoing the process in the National Health Service. It is also true that more than half have to seek abortions outside the NHS either because there is no service in their area, or that service is unacceptably slow, unpleasant or punitive. I doubt the same can be said of any other medical service.

For women to understand that others feel as they do is clearly helpful as the taboo surrounding abortion makes it still harder to talk after than before the event. Equally, it is helpful for women to realize that the intense feelings with which they may feel trapped, after an abortion, are not a life sentence. Only a very small number of women continue to have bad feelings for a long time after the operation. Caroline, a mother of three children who had an abortion two years ago, says:

> I thought about my abortion every day, then after about a year I had a very busy phase – a couple of the kids changed school and my husband started a new job, and I realized after about six weeks that I just hadn't thought about the abortion. But that made me feel dreadful. I

went into an awful depressed guilty state and I made myself think and think about it.

Then in the end I rang a friend who had been kind before and went to talk to her because I felt so bad. She just said to me that I was indulging myself. She was really tough on me because she said I had made a decision, gone through it and I had suffered a lot of grief and that was enough. I remember her words, 'If you had to pay any dues you have done it. Now let the thing go and get on with leading a constructive life.' In fact she reduced me to tears; I think I was shocked being talked to like that, but I bless her for it because she made me think and yes, I was able to let go then.

Brenda remembers the difficulty of adjusting back to the state of not being pregnant:

In a curious way I had felt a sense of companionship with the foetus. It was horrid because I knew it had to go, but all the same I felt I had company with me for the six weeks it was there. So after the operation instead of just getting on with life again, I found myself missing this companionship and going back all the time to remembering the feeling. That made it hard.

For some women the time when the baby would have been born is a watershed. After this date they can begin to let the experience go, although some find the feelings about the abortion will recur at each anniversary.

Greta: I felt that somehow the foetus was still part of me, part of my existence during the time it would have grown to be a viable child. In a way that is rather horrid because of course it didn't grow, but I have this feeling that there is a spirit and although it cannot grow on this earth, in this life, it still exists. For me the date of birth was the time I could relinquish responsibility for that spirit.

Women who do not feel they have the right to choose to end the life of the foetus, but have done so because they could see no alternative, suffer considerably more than those who may wish they had not had to make the choice, who may regret not being able to have a baby, but who feel it was a morally legitimate choice. Louise, who had her third child aborted because her husband issued an ultimatum, is convinced that she will never escape the feeling that she killed her child: 'I relive that ten days or so even though it was eight years ago. I live in fear of something dreadful happening to the two children I have.' Jenny, who chose abortion because she felt another child would deprive her other children of the time and attention they needed, felt 'glad' her operation went wrong and she 'paid' for the abortion:

> While they were performing my abortion something happened and they managed to damage me inside. It ended up with an emergency hysterectomy. Of course it was horrifying and I was very shocked at first, but then I felt a kind of relief. I felt that I had paid for having aborted that child; it seemed that God was punishing me and that it was His way of allowing me to let the experience go.

Discussion of the distress and sadness that women may feel at their abortion is often used by anti-abortionists as evidence that abortion is too easily obtained, that women would be happier if it were not offered to them as an option and they had to have their babies.

This argument fails to take into account that women who take the very serious step of requesting the termination of a pregnancy do not do so lightly, but understand the seriousness of what they choose to do. What they are doing in admitting ambivalence and distress is saying that it is possible to make a decision which is right and yet involves conflict and pain.

Forcing women to have babies they have decided they cannot cope with, by making it impossibly hard for them to get terminations, does not make the women happier and can lead to active resentment of the child. This is confirmed by several detailed pieces of research. A study on the outcome of induced abortion, made by Raymond Illsley and Marion Hall, states: 'Reports of adverse emotional reactions following induced abortion have often ignored the possibility that adverse reactions can also result from refusal of abortion. Detailed and complete studies have uncovered considerable distress and dissatisfaction among women who were refused abortion.'[34] And pointing to a number of studies where a high percentage of the number of women have regretted that they did not get abortions and have attempted suicide or shown symptoms of severe depression, they note: 'It seems that although many women who are refused abortion adjust to their situation and grow to love the child, about half would still have preferred abortion, a large minority suffer considerable distress, and a small minority develop severe disturbance.'

Pare and Raven, in their study of 321 patients referred for consideration of abortion, write: 'Termination of pregnancy caused little psychiatric disturbance provided the patient wanted an abortion; continuation of pregnancy, however, did on occasion lead to serious psychiatric disability, and a third of the mothers who kept their babies showed evidence of resenting them.'[35] Of women who were refused termination after a psychiatric consultation, 34 per cent regretted the decision and four had serious psychiatric illness. Of 28 who were refused without a psychiatric opinion, three had severe adverse reactions. Pare and Raven also note: 'One-third of the women in this series showed evidence of resenting their babies.'

While the material gathered from the 150 women contacted for this book revealed plenty of sadness and distress, there were very few who in the end felt that termination had been the wrong decision. Of the few who did feel this way, in three cases it was because the women saw the pregnancy as their last chance to have a child; another five felt that the grief they endured over a long time was worse than any struggle they would have had in bringing up an unplanned child. One was a woman in her late twenties who had become pregnant by a man she was having an affair with and had decided on abortion because she had a new job to go to. But as the job fell through immediately after the abortion, she was suffering a profound sense of loss and felt that she should not have 'gambled' on the job and that having the baby would have avoided the distress she felt.

Among the other women there were varied feelings ranging from those who expressed no real sadness to those who found themselves unexpectedly upset and those who, having broken a lifelong set of moral beliefs, found themselves having to come to terms with the recognition that the simplicity of clear-cut right and wrong no longer existed for them.

> Nina: I had always felt that abortion wasn't right; I used to tut-tut when I read articles about it – that sort of thing. So when I got pregnant and ended up making that choice, it was a real shock. And afterwards I felt sort of humble – I knew I wasn't the same person any more. I couldn't judge others any more and I had to start thinking about lots of other things like bombs, eating meat – oh all sorts of things I had had set ideas about.

Sarah, who was 19 when she got pregnant by her boyfriend who she felt was 'too immature for fatherhood', remembers the anguish she felt when, returning to work after her abortion, she began producing milk: 'That broke me up, I cried and cried thinking that the baby should have been drinking it. But the milk stopped and the feelings got slowly better. It took time but it happened. Now I look back and I still feel sad but in retrospect I can say I made the right

decision in spite of regretting it immediately afterwards.'
Mandy had her abortion three years ago:

I believe you must put the past behind you, but this is one
part of my life which will never be forgotten. I am
reminded every day by seeing babies on the street or on
TV. This is further complicated by the fact that I work as
a cleaner once a week at the flat of the local LIFE
president so I am reminded by the posters and leaflets
there.

I often wonder what my child would have looked like
but I have no regrets about my decision, only remorse. I
know I made the right decision but I feel remorse that it
ever happened in the first place.

As to religious beliefs, I am confused. I believe
children are a gift from God so I was wrong in destroying
that potential life, or was I right in thinking that every
child has a right to live only under certain conditions –
i.e. to be wanted and to be brought up under the
guidance of both father and mother? I'm sure my
confusion is made worse by my feeling of isolation, with
not coming into contact with anyone who has been in
the same dilemma as myself.

Marianne's husband had died shortly before she became
involved with a married man.

I shocked myself because I never thought I would get
involved with anyone married, but I was very low and
desperate at the time. Life without my husband was
dreadful and we had only been married a short time.

This man kept saying he wanted to leave his home and
live with me, but he never did of course. But he talked a
lot about how his wife wanted to get pregnant and
couldn't and I think I became careless about
contraception, thinking – although it wasn't conscious –
that if I got pregnant I would be in a stronger position
than the wife.

Looking back it seems dreadfully callous and irresponsible but that was the state I was in. Then when I did get pregnant and told him, he couldn't cope at all. At first he was going to leave and we would be a family, then he felt he couldn't because that would be so tough on his wife, that she would feel she had failed because she couldn't have a child.

The mad thing was that in the middle of all this the baby became almost incidental. I don't know that either of us really thought about it as a real thing, just a bargaining object.

Anyhow this went on for about a month and then, suddenly, I just decided it was hopeless. I suppose I could see that he wasn't going to make any commitment to me or the baby. Yet knowing the kind of man he was, I knew he would want to keep seeing it, to have some kind of contact. So it seemed to me that I would never be free of him if I had the child, but I would never have him either.

In fact when I said I would have the abortion, he was mighty relieved and became much nicer to me, very supportive and caring – ironic really.

Straight after the abortion I didn't feel much, but then after a couple of months it hit me – this great sense of loss. I had lost him because although he was still around a bit, we both knew it was over. I had lost the baby and I had lost some of my self-esteem. It was awful and I became terribly depressed.

I went to a therapist which was helpful because I was focusing everything on losing the child which was madness really because I loathe the idea of being a single mother and I don't doubt that I made the right choice; I honestly wouldn't have been a good mother in the circumstances. Instead I needed to work out how I was going to get my life straight and run it properly in the future.

So although I did go through a lot of pain about the abortion, I also feel it allowed me to get out of a very destructive situation. It sounds harsh in some ways as though that foetus had no right to consideration in its own right, but I honestly cannot see a tiny foetus as being developed mentally and emotionally enough to have rights.

That many of the women who volunteered to come forward and talk intimately and openly about their experiences for this book, said that it was the first time they had been able to do so gives some indication of how powerfully the taboo on the subject silences women. For these were women who clearly wanted to talk but who felt trapped with their feelings, who dared not admit the confused feelings they had to anyone they knew, and most of all felt they had no right to ask for sympathy and compassion. A married woman who had terminated a pregnancy by the husband who walked out on her when she told him she was pregnant, says: 'If I looked logically at the situation it seemed to me I made the decision which had to be made – that if anyone was forcing the abortion it was him. But the fact is the life was growing in my body, I ultimately made the choice about ending it, so I didn't feel I could go to people and say how sad I felt.'

Yet where does this belief that a woman has committed so fundamental a wrong that she may not be allowed normal grief come from? It tends to be attributed to the church, which to many believers offers final condemnation of abortion. However, the church is not so absolute. The organization Christians for a Free Choice argues with conviction for a woman's right to choose, while individual members of the church have stated that abortion must ultimately be a matter for the individual conscience, not an absolute of theological doctrine. Dr John Robinson writes, 'The Christian, more than anyone else must start from what "is" in a non-moralistic, non-judgemental way . . . In the last resort the right to decide must rest . . . with the mother herself.'[36] The Very Reverend Edward Patey, Dean of Liverpool, has said: 'This is an area where God has put a moral choice in men's [sic] hands, and this choice must be exercised as responsibly as possible for the well-being both of the individual and the community. In the exercise of this choice there can be no moral absolutes.'[37]

Even Roman Catholics, generally thought to be opposed to abortion by definition, have formed a group, Catholics for a Free Choice, which believes that 'abortion is a serious moral problem and while we are not "for abortion", we nonetheless believe that in true charity and Christian conscience there are many serious reasons that we should justify this act.' Sara Maitland, an Anglo-Catholic, believes:

> It is hypocritical for the church to take this very rigorous sanctity of human life attitude about the foetus and then not take it elsewhere. Apart from the Quakers, there is no other church which has committed itself absolutely to pacifism. It seems to me that to be able to say that it is possible to drop a nuclear bomb on thousands – millions – of innocent people is permissible in certain circumstances, but that it is never possible to abort a baby whatever the circumstances, is a position of moral shabbiness.
>
> The real problem is a social problem, a reason why I wouldn't want to see the Abortion Law repealed because it does seem to me that it is the mother who has to carry the pain, all the emotional burden and most of the physical one, and if she decides she can't do it then it is nobody's business to tell her that she can jolly well pull herself together and have the child because Jesus loves her.
>
> If Jesus loves her then why the hell isn't she getting more support? It is one more sign of the sexism of things

that so many women need to do this thing. They need to do it because society is bloody to mothers and babies and because the medical profession will not service our most primary demand which is for contraception which works.

Looked at like this, I cannot see why women must be looked at as solitary sinners if they choose abortion.

Unfortunately, this kind of thinking and questioning is often not available to women who feel flawed and guilty, and entitled to no grief. And so often it is the idea that they have sinned in the eyes of God that prevents women from expressing the kind of grief which is encouraged in the face of any other kind of death. One woman talking of her time in a mixed gynaecological ward expresses this poignantly: 'There was a woman next to me who was losing her baby and the nurse made a great fuss of her. But she just ignored me. Nobody cared that I was losing my baby; that wasn't considered a tragedy.'

The importance of understanding and support throughout the experience of abortion is recognized by many people committed to a woman's right to choose. One senior counsellor for a large charity describes her own approach:

I always say to a client, however old or young, or whatever the circumstances, that she will grieve for what has had to happen. It is the one death that you know is going to take place at a certain hour in a certain place.

In a sense we are all involved in bereavement counselling. I think it is of supreme importance to warn a woman in advance of what she might feel later on. Because I think for lots of women who have got kids, who work, whose lives are busy, pragmatism takes over. They get up and get going again, but what can happen is that the shock then takes place later, which I think happens with a lot of older women. That can happen days, weeks, months, maybe years later.

I think it hits them less if they have the chance to really deliberate about what they are doing, but I still think most women grieve and I think it is absolutely vital that they should be allowed to do so; that they should allow themselves to do so. Regret is integral to the whole experience. It is a necessary part of rehabilitation, of getting back to 'normality'. It's part of establishing the state of not being pregnant again and re-establishing equilibrium. When you are no longer physically pregnant you have to come to terms with it mentally and emotionally.

It helps a good deal if a woman has a caring partner or close friend she can talk to about her feelings before and after the abortion. But for many women there is no such friend. So what kind of help can they seek if they long to talk but can find no-one to listen?

The charities performing private abortions usually have counsellors who are very willing to see women after their terminations, and many offer to make appointments at the time the abortion is arranged. But few women keep these appointments and the general view is that women do not feel comfortable about returning to the place where the abortion was set up.

A more successful idea appears to be therapeutic groups where women can meet together informally to talk through their experience, listen to what other women have to say and in some cases participate in exercises designed to help unravel any areas of repressed feelings. Mira Dana, who suffered considerable anguish over her own abortion experience some years ago, helped to set up a woman's post-abortion workshop at the Women's Therapy Centre in London. She began from an intimate knowledge of the problems and emotions which surround the experience of abortion and it was only through talking and sharing her feelings that she found she was able to come to terms with what happened. She says:

By breaking the secrecy and silence and by acknowledging the feelings involved you can reduce the torment of having to cope with them on your own and the sense of isolation you may have experienced whilst confused about your feelings and thinking you are the only person in the world who feels this way.

Abortion is a taboo subject. As a woman who has just gone through the experience you are faced with an unbearable situation. Often overwhelmed with unfamiliar feelings, you are not able to talk about it with others. Often, no-one has prepared you for what is going to happen to you, either physically or emotionally.

As the subject is either unmentioned or talked about with harsh judgement, you carry the feeling that you will be judged and blamed for it. Support is what you need most and you are often unable to ask for it because of the shame involved.

In the workshops she runs, Mira asks each woman individually to talk about what happened to her, what her feelings were and are, how she felt she was treated. Because the workshop includes a full day's session, women have time to tell their tale slowly and in as much detail as they wish. They are encouraged to be as sad or as angry as they wish and many women cry for the first time in this environment. Mira explains:

So many women just feel they are alone, that there isn't anyone who will understand what they are going through, who they trust not to hold the knowledge against them. But in the groups women know they have all made the same choice, committed the same 'sin' or however they see it, and when they begin to talk and recognize that the other women are caring and supportive it can act as a watershed for feelings which have been pent up a long time.

We get women coming who have just had abortions,

but also women who have bottled up their feelings for years and hear about us by chance. We see women who have apparently had no problem in having an abortion and it is only years later that they begin to realize the impact it had.

Because abortion has become more freely available, it is sometimes fashionable and liberal to think of it as a minor event in a woman's life. One woman I remember said: 'I have written in my diary: Friday – 1. Put car in garage. 2. Abortion. 3. Shopping. 4. Take car out of garage. Not until four years later did I realize the full importance of what it meant for me to have had it.'

From watching such feelings being unleashed Mira has come to feel that this flippant attitude is 'almost as dangerous as that which seeks to claim that abortion is murder and, therefore, should not be available'. She says: 'There is no way of avoiding the issue of an abortion being the termination of a potential human life and the feelings that this brings up for you. It is precisely these feelings that are denied by the current liberal view of it as being a minor event.' It was Mira Dana's workshops which provided the model for a booklet issued at the first showing of the film *Mixed Feelings*. And although many people did set up groups, most ended when the women felt they had got all they wanted from the group.

Ruth was one of a number of Leicester women who formed a self-help group after seeing *Mixed Feelings*. She advertised for women interested in joining a group and had a response from half a dozen women. They met for several weeks and during this time talked through the experiences they had had, looked at their relationships, contacts with their parents, the way friends had reacted. Ruth says:

We were different ages, different circumstances and different classes, but that didn't matter. We had come to share our common experience and that was valuable. At first it wasn't easy. Nobody actually wanted to open up to begin with, but then one of the women did and then things began to flow.

The good thing was that, besides grief and regret which were certainly brought out, women also got very angry and shouted and swore which was very exciting and cathartic. There was also a good deal of humour. Once we got to the angry, noisy stage women started finding they could make jokes about things which had just seemed dreadful before.

The group went on for several weeks which was as long as any of us wanted. We didn't try to carry it on because none of us had time to be a leader for other people, but I now think it would be good to try to set up an ongoing structure.

I know the group made a lot of difference to me. I felt very alone after my abortion although my circumstances weren't particularly bad. But the group allowed me to put the experience away. I don't feel anything much about it any more.

Hilary went to a post-abortion group because, she says, 'I was feeling weak and horrible. My husband had a job and I was just on the dole, doing nothing. I used to get very sad and cry for no apparent reason. I went to the discussion group and all the women there were women who had had abortions. It was just for an evening and I think that was very helpful because I really wanted to talk about it with someone who'd actually been through it.' Joan wished there had been somewhere to go after her abortion, to talk with other women. She says:

I actually thought of setting up a group myself. I used to belong to a women's group and they were all pro-abortion, but I didn't share the way they felt about it. I had suffered over the abortion, I felt damaged by it and not exactly jubilant at having had the opportunity to exercise this right to choose. So I didn't need the heavy, political support. I really wanted people who felt the ambivalences as I did and who felt regret as I did.

In a way it was this issue which brought me into conflict with the women's movement. I had always been involved with issues and groups before and I was as political as anyone but I suppose I realized that the business of abortion is much more complicated for women than just a legal right.

Other women have expressed similar feelings and it is quite clear there is here a dilemma for feminism. On the one hand, it is essential that the struggle for abortion for those women who want it must continue. As the moral climate becomes more reactionary and anti-abortionists work hard to have the Abortion Act repealed, there is a very real danger of a return to a situation where women are forced to bear children they feel they cannot cope with, or resort to back-street abortions. On the other hand, it is important that the political battle for this right should not gag women, making them feel they must not speak out about their ambivalent feelings since these can be taken as reasons for preventing abortion being available. Women who have campaigned for the right to choose need now to acknowledge that having ambivalent, distressing feelings is a legitimate part of the experience and in no way undermines the importance of allowing women who feel they need an abortion to have it with the minimum of trauma. That some women who have been involved in the long and difficult battle to get the Abortion Act brought in do not always understand or wish to confront the distressing aftermath which can follow abortion is understandable, because in the early days of the struggle any indication that it was not an absolutely right decision for women, would have been used as hostile propaganda. Equally, concern with the central issue may have imposed a certain blindness or single-mindedness on those who were working hard for change.

Yet the taboo on abortion is forceful enough without feminists who, while supporting women by fighting for the right to choose, sometimes make it hard for them to express their negative feelings.

Breaking this taboo is an important part of helping women to take responsibility for their lives, to live honestly with their actions. The difficulty of speaking out undoubtedly causes many women great distress. If women are encouraged to speak out about what the right to choose means to them on an individual level, not only will it help to exorcize the feelings they experience as forbidden, but it will also allow them to help us understand their reasons for choosing termination.

Speaking out also means that women can reveal not just the negative side but also the positive things which many – even if they have suffered a good deal – ultimately see as having come as a result of the abortion. Some of the women who spoke to us about their abortion described the pleasure of finding a strength they had not believed they possessed. Others felt that the conflict experienced before the abortion had helped them see clearly what they valued in their lives. No-one would choose abortion as a growth experience, but this is precisely what it is for many women, particularly those who have never before been expected to take a major decision, who have spent their lives being dependent and playing a passive role whether as a wife and mother or as a working woman with limited job aspirations. It is all too common for women, whose passivity and lack of assertiveness are so often encouraged in the name of femininity, to have little or no reason to confront the issues of control, morality and responsibility over their lives. Confronted with an unplanned pregnancy, they cannot avoid the decision. Even the most caring and supportive man is not able to take on that responsibility for a woman. She has to make the decision and come to terms with it on her own.

It is a lonely experience for many women:

> My partner stood by me all the way and he really did
> recognize that it was half his responsibility, and yet I
> knew deep down that I was on my own. I could if I
> wanted decide to have the kid and if I chose abortion I
> would have to go through with it all by myself.
>
> I didn't like it. My first inclination was to just not
> think. But that wasn't possible of course and I found,
> about three months after the termination, that I felt a
> confidence in myself I hadn't had before. I found too
> that I didn't need to play the 'little girl', the helpless
> female to my partner so much.

For Marianne, the knowledge that she could survive an
ordeal which caused her enormous emotional upset, was
important:

> When I first had the abortion I thought I was going to
> crack up. There seemed to be no place to turn to in my
> life where there wasn't pain. With my husband dead, my
> lover gone and the emptiness of having decided it was
> the wrong time for a baby, I felt as though everything was
> falling apart.
>
> And for several weeks I think I was quite crazy and for
> a short time I contemplated trying to get pregnant again
> – thank goodness some kind of rationality took over. I
> suppose though that there was quite a strong survival
> instinct in me. I kept working and to all outside
> purposes, I appeared to function well.
>
> And as time passed the rational bit came more and
> more to the fore and I actually became aware of
> recovering. It was a surprise to realize that yes, I was
> going to get over it.
>
> And I have. I can honestly say it doesn't worry me any
> more and it is knowing that I have got through a crisis
> which seemed so severe, so intense, that makes me feel

strong. I do feel that I have learned to survive and I cherish that.

Alice, who is married with two children and had an abortion two years ago because she and her husband decided they could not manage another child, went through a time of feeling she was quite unlovable.

I felt that I had done something bad and that nobody could possibly love me if they knew me inside. It was horrible because there were no friends or family to talk with and who might have shown that they still did care for me.

In the end I went to a priest who was very kindly and helpful and he didn't condemn me but said, 'God makes these rules so we don't hurt ourselves' – he felt I had made the wrong decision for me.

I'm not so sure, but even thinking the decision was right didn't take away the unpleasant feelings. But it made me try very very hard to be good to the kids, to give them more time and attention than I had before, and I put more effort into my marriage too. In a way I wanted to compensate for killing a potential child by giving the living people in my family more of me.

And of course that does bring rewards. I began to get closer to the kids, things improved with my husband and me and I felt that in a way I had learnt how important these things are.

Lisa: I had to organize the whole thing myself and although I cried a lot after and couldn't look at babies – all that sort of thing – I felt a kind of pride in myself for actually having sorted out the whole thing. I felt I was able to do things in a way I hadn't felt before.

Linda has had a variety of feelings since her abortion – exhilaration and relief immediately it was over; some grief after that; and now, a year and a half later, she says: 'I feel that I can accept what I've done. I don't regret it at all. I feel that I gained strength from it. And I feel that because I have gone through something that only women can go through, my commitment to the women's movement has increased.'

Jenny was 21 when she got pregnant by a man she intended to marry but who was not yet in a position to 'commit himself'. She had her abortion through BPAS and felt supported and comforted all the way through. She has emerged with strong, positive feelings: 'Emotionally I'm a much stronger person now. The experience has made me take more control of my life. When I give up my job, I intend to take up some voluntary work and I will apply for a post with the local BPAS or a young people's advisory service. I feel that my experience needs to be shared.'

The time after an abortion is, then, a period when women may go through many different emotions and sensations. While some certainly have few if any distressing feelings, it is clear that a great many women suffer a good deal and that to suffer is a normal part of the process of assimilation and recovery.

Most of the women who got in touch with us were able to talk with detachment of their experience. And while some said they would never – nor felt they should – forget the experience, they also spoke with relief of how the intense feelings had subsided, even though they had imagined at first they never would.

9. Men and Abortion

Men do not talk much about abortion. Without them, there would be no unplanned pregnancy or termination, yet this is not reflected in the experience of abortion. The discussion, the debate, the anguish, the practical issues surrounding abortion are not generally shared by men except as doctors. Men all too often do not apparently accept the moral responsibility for their actions.

Indeed, very often men occupy a peripheral role when the woman who has become pregnant by them has a termination. Why is this? There are a number of stereotypes of men faced with an abortion: the 'scoundrel' who runs off when he hears his woman is pregnant, who denies it can be his or refuses to discuss it; the man who offers to pay as a way of absolving himself from responsibility; the man who helps the girlfriend through 'her' nasty experience. And, of course, the married men who do not want a child and threaten to leave home if the wife will not terminate the pregnancy. But these stereotypes do not help us understand the feelings and behaviour of the many men who want to be supportive.

For all the men who take off, who blame the woman for not coping with contraception properly, who withdraw from responsibility and emotional involvement, who ignore the feelings the woman has about abortion because they do not want a child, there are men who want to support the woman, who have deep feelings about the pregnancy and abortion and who want to take a more positive and supportive role.

In writing this book we felt it important to record the views of the men involved. So we asked partners of women, who were willing to talk, to give their version of the experience. We also advertised for men to come forward with their feelings and responses to abortions. This brought about 30 men in all, a tiny amount compared with the 200-odd women who volunteered their experiences in response to letters in magazines and papers around the country. And whereas the women who responded were of different class, creed and colour, the men were mostly middle-class and white and had basically sought to involve themselves and support their woman, although one speaks retrospectively of the guilt he feels at telling his girlfriend he would leave if she had the baby, and another feels bad at 'forcing' himself on his girlfriend the night she got pregnant. It is a shame that those men whom women describe with seemingly justifiable bitterness, who left them, changed from passionate lovers into indifferent acquaintances, put their own interests before any consideration of the woman's, did not come forward. For there may be a rationalization, an explanation of such behaviour which would be enlightening and valuable.

The difficulty of getting a broad-based picture of male feelings was shared by the American sociologist Arthur Shostak and his co-authors Gary McLouth and Lyn Seng in *Men and Abortion: Lessons in Love*[39]. He acknowledges that the interviewees for his book were primarily loving, caring individuals who had taken their women to the clinic and tried to be emotionally supportive at the time of the abortion.

While they may not have been a good cross-section, the men who did come forward spoke openly and apparently honestly and the things they had to say were illuminating and in some cases presented an insight into feelings which would probably have been helpful to the women concerned at the time. And repeatedly they expressed dismay at feeling that there was no positive, constructive role for them to play in the abortion experience. They were not sure how much right they had to express a desire for the child or to demonstrate grief at making the choice of abortion; some worried whether it was reasonable to make it known that they did not want the child. Interviewed in the *Sunday Times*, Jeremy Cattell described how after his girlfriend had an abortion he cried himself to sleep, was unable to concentrate at work and felt guilty. Talking to other men, he found them suffering similarly and he said: 'I felt anguish and I was incredibly angry. That baby had an awful lot to do with me and I wanted it badly. I'm convinced I'm not a freak, that this is a common experience for men but they are not prepared to voice it. They hide behind a macho front and don't let their true feelings take hold. They are afraid of feminists, afraid to challenge a woman's argument, 'It's my body, my choice.'

A hard-line 'woman's right to choose' position does not leave an obvious place for men to express any feelings. Peter, one of our interviewees, said:

> My girlfriend and I discussed abortion and I think we both agreed that it was the right thing, but then I felt very much that she took it on as her responsibility, her ordeal and that I was not wanted. She insisted on going to the clinic alone although I would happily have gone too.
>
> But she did rely a lot on her girlfriends and I felt very strongly that she saw it as a woman's concern. The fact that I was the father became sort of unimportant.

But if it is not a woman's right to choose, whose is it? Can a man be given the right to dictate that a woman must bear a child she does not want? Clearly there are men who believe so. Cases have been brought to court here and in America by men who want their women to be prevented from having terminations. In all these cases the courts have ruled that, ultimately, a woman cannot be expected to bear a child she does not want, which surely has to be right although if causes hurt in cases such as that of Martin who was prepared to take the child and bring it up without the mother. He says:

I loved the girl very much and so much wanted the child we had made together. But she was devastated at the idea of what a nine-month pregnancy would mean in her life – she was just beginning to work, to be independent – at that time and although she did think about what I suggested, in the end she said no. I was very upset but I suppose that's the way nature made things and it wouldn't be right for the law to try to force women to have babies.

However, such situations are not common. For all the men genuinely prepared to take on the task of bringing up a child on their own, far more take a proprietorial line on the 'morality' of aborting 'their' child without contemplating the idea of sharing the bringing up of the child. Christine recalls: 'I was pregnant and my boyfriend got furious when I talked about abortion. But then when I asked if he was prepared to marry me and be a family man, he made it very plain he wasn't. I've seen it with friends too – there's a lot of double standards around.'

Or there are men who dissuade their women from abortion by offering to share the responsibility – but duck out of that responsibility later. As Lesley found:

I had a job and a flat when I started having an affair with Bob. When I got pregnant I could see it would mean sacrificing my career, and my landlord insisted on more rent because I would have a baby. Bob didn't suggest living together but he did say he would be around and would help and contribute to the baby. It didn't sound great to me but the fact that he seemed to want the baby swung me round to having her.

Then after a few months he got bored. He said he found it boring, that I got on at him all the time. Then we had a big row and he got together with another girl and here I am a single mum. Well, I wouldn't be without the baby now because how could you ever not want your child? But I do know I would have chosen to have children at a better time in life. This is very hard and I don't know how I'll ever manage to get a decent job. So I suppose we'll always be poor, living on the state.

Even when men are with their partners and want the child, how often do they honestly share the responsibility? How many are prepared to give up a career, a life style to have an unplanned child? Judging by the proportion of childcare that is shouldered by women, even in planned families, the answer has to be not many. We are all caught in cultural patterns, in living modes which suit the way society operates, but the fact that a pregnant woman must contemplate responsibility for a new human being, with all that that entails, makes it clear that she should be the person who ultimately decides whether or not to have a child.

This is one perspective on the reason abortion has become an issue of woman's choice. Another reason that organizations such as the National Abortion Campaign and the Women's Rights Reproductive Information Centre see it as vital that women do maintain a position of strength is the control that a male-dominated medical profession and male-dominated policy-makers hold over deciding whether they shall or shall not be allowed to say what happens to their bodies. As an organizer at the WRRIC said:

> Women have to go to doctors, almost always male, to beg permission to have an abortion; they have to petition a primarily male parliament to have an abortion law which permits them to have a choice about the children they bear.
>
> In a society where we do not need more children, where women are expected to take on the job of bringing up the next generation, it is absolute nonsense that men should be in the position to decide the fate of a woman's life. So yes, it is vital that women see abortion as their issue. It may be hard on some men; there will be

injustices but those injustices are not as great as the injustice to women which men too often exercise when given dominance over them.

But while it is understandable that the abortion issue is a battlefield with war being waged for female control, there is little doubt that many women would benefit if more men were prepared to share the experience, to express their feelings, to open up and when they do it is important to listen. So the interviews with men who did come forward are presented fully, to give context and substance to what they are saying, and because they are the few willing to open up and give information.

Robert, a former teacher, is white and his girlfriend is a black health worker.

In the month we had been together we had become very attached to each other, but we certainly hadn't discussed settling down together, although she was spending most of the time at my flat. So when she missed her period and found she was pregnant it was a shock, certainly not something that fitted in well. My girlfriend was training in her work and didn't want to give all that up, and the whole thing was further complicated by the fact that she is black, that we would have a mixed-race child which is something, I believe, needs careful thinking about. I didn't feel it was an issue we had discussed.

My girlfriend was very well-informed when it came to knowing how to get a termination and on the surface things were fine. I supported her by paying half, taking her to the clinic and being around to talk to before, and she seemed to be glad of that. But then when she went in I began to feel on the one hand very inadequate, that I wasn't really going through it with her, and rationally I knew that was how it had to be, but on another level I felt very excluded. I felt that I wanted to suffer, to share responsibility and there wasn't a place for me.

I also felt very sad, a deep melancholy and a sense of failure that I couldn't have wanted the child and the woman enough to make it all alright. And although it didn't show then I think she felt a bit the same – that our relationship wasn't big enough to have transcended what happened. It's a bit strange, because we made the decision together but after that the sense of being together seemed to disintegrate.

After the abortion she was numb and quite ill and she stayed at my place. But there was a sort of resentment I felt, a pressure which wasn't spoken but which quite definitely came into our relationship. For me I'm sure it was guilt; I felt bad about having got her pregnant, having put her through an abortion and it wasn't something I could really talk about with her. I felt she had been so organized, so sure about setting it all up that my reaction was a bit inappropriate.

It would have been good to talk to somebody about it. I do have a man friend and I told him briefly that she was having an abortion, so then he said yes, it's happened to me. But he wouldn't talk about it. I wish there was some kind of help, some group for men. I know I would have liked that.

Gordon, a local government employee, had been married for five years. When his marriage broke up he started an affair with a woman, considerably younger than he is, who already had a small son.

Things were difficult because she always had to go home to her Mum when we met so we decided to live together – probably sooner than was sensible. Our sex life wasn't particularly good but she did get pregnant very quickly. I was using a Durex and it was obviously bad luck. In fact I felt rather pleased, I suppose I felt ready to have a child, and I would have married her. But she was distraught. She already had a child and seemed very upset and angry.

So I acquiesced when she said she wanted to have an abortion; I just accepted what she wanted although I wasn't at all happy about it, but I suppose I was a coward. I didn't want to be rejected by her saying she didn't want to be with me and have my child, so I agreed that yes she was right and I thought that if I accepted what she wanted then it would keep our relationship going.

But actually our relationship deteriorated badly. She didn't want me around and we didn't sleep together any more. I think she was frightened about the abortion, but I found it hard to work out exactly what she felt because she didn't seem to want to talk about it and I just thought she was being very cool, very composed. And then I found, after a month, that she hadn't done anything about fixing the abortion so at this point I took over and took her to hospital for an appointment. I pushed aside any thoughts of it being my baby and that I might keep it.

I wasn't being noble – really the opposite. I was very concerned at the idea of the relationship breaking up and I wanted to help her. Looking back I wonder if I was right, if she really did want to go ahead, whether she would have liked me to express some positive feelings. It haunts me, the idea that I might have misread her. It seemed so certain from what she said that she knew her mind, and I'm not much good at expressing emotions or my own feelings. But yes, I wonder a lot now if I should have been more positive about what I felt.

As it was, things went very smoothly. She was given an NHS abortion with no trouble but when I went in to see her she burst into tears and was very angry that I had come. That hurt a lot but she really meant it. She wouldn't let me collect her and afterwards she went and stayed with her mum. I wanted to talk to her about it all but she didn't and then our relationship split up. Yes, I have a lot of regrets now. I don't think what we did was right and I wouldn't want to do it again, but I think looking back that I didn't know what to do, there isn't a definite part a man plays, there aren't certain things expected, you are left to try to feel your way and get it right.

Mike, a graduate with a busy career, had been living with Jane, who worked in a shop and had no interest in her job, for several years. She had been talking for some time about wanting children. He had not felt ready although he had a distant idea that they would together raise a family.

It was her birthday the night it happened. We had been drinking a lot and I don't know if she was using her cap or not, but when she told me she was pregnant I was very angry, I felt I was being manipulated and I didn't like it. I was young at the time and I didn't have any feelings about it being my responsibility.

I very much believed in the business about a woman's right to choose; I supported that idea utterly and in a way I think that prevented me from thinking about what abortion actually means, and particularly about what it would mean to Jane. I just assumed an abortion would sort things out.

I knew she didn't like the idea much, but it never occurred to me that I was being brutal by assuming it was the right thing. In fact I gave her an ultimatum between me and the baby. Thinking back I can see how hideously insensitive that was, but at the time I didn't think in those terms. I just had in my mind that I would resent the child for the rest of my life if we had it and stayed together. So no, I didn't talk things through with Jane and when she saw I was serious about the relationship ending if she had the child, she agreed to abortion, and she appeared to agree rationally with my arguments.

She was fairly weepy when she got home afterwards and I assumed it was like postnatal depression and would soon pass. As far as I was concerned we could get back to normal, there was nothing more to be said. But it didn't pass and she became badly depressed; we had some terrible downs and arguments, and then manic highs, but I really couldn't see how it connected to the abortion. By now she was urging me to get married; she very much wanted babies and I thought we might as well do it. So then almost immediately she got pregnant and this time I felt glad, it seemed right and I felt ready to take responsibility. It made all the difference to her – it was as though she could put the abortion behind her once the baby was born.

We had another child and adopted one more but the marriage didn't last in the end; I don't think it would have with or without the abortion. The abortion stopped bothering Jane but I have thought about it and about my behaviour a lot since.

At college, Julian had a relationship with a girl in his year. He was 19 at the time, she 16.

When she got home one holiday she phoned to say that she was pregnant. I felt panic but after that I felt quite good about it. Of course a bit of that was knowing I was 'a real male', that I was potent, but I also felt it would cement our relationship.

So I went off to see her in this frame of mind, but when I got to her home her mother was there and furious. She wouldn't let me see Barbara. I really didn't want her to have an abortion and I wanted the chance to talk with her, but I couldn't and when I phoned she was very cold and distant.

I suppose her parents put pressure on her not to have anything to do with me. I was terribly worried about her; I felt I should be there but that wasn't how it was seen by her parents. The idea that it was half my situation, my responsibility didn't come in to it. I was just the bad guy.

And I never saw her again. I heard from her tutor that she had left the course and I wasn't able to reach her on the phone. It was very weird knowing that she had been carrying my child, that she had had an abortion, and feeling sure I ought to be there to comfort her, but not being there and not having any idea how she was.

And it was the beginning of a lot of problems. Everything was unfinished, unresolved for me. The idea that men don't feel much about abortion is rubbish. I found I couldn't study and I began taking drugs, then at the time when the child would have been born I started having a curious vision. I had the very strong impression that there was a child nearby and I felt absolutely sure it was a son. And this became more and more prominent. I began to see him clearly, at the end of my bed.

And the weird thing was as time went on he grew, he seemed to get older as he would have done if he had been real. I thought it was a ghost and, strangely I didn't connect it with the abortion, but then I began to realize that that was what it was.

I felt immensely sad and guilty and it went on for years. There was one occasion I recall very clearly, when he seemed to look at me with such remorse. I didn't talk about it with the girlfriend I had then because I don't think she would have liked it – I think she would have felt jealous of the depth of the relationship before. So I bottled everything up and my own problems got worse. I found making love I was often impotent.

It was not until about ten years later, when I began living with a very sympathetic, caring girl who I could talk to about it all, that things improved. I started having the vision less often and, curiously, I found I missed seeing him. It was all very strange and disturbing and then when I was splitting up with this girl it all came back and I woke up screaming one night. And that was the end. He never came back.

It all made me very against abortion for a while, but
that hasn't lasted because I don't think banning abortion
is the answer, and I don't think it was necessarily the
answer to my situation. Who knows, if she had had the
child what would have happened.

If I could have talked to someone who would have
understood that I was grieving – because I'm sure I was
for the child and the loss of the relationship – it would
have helped a lot. I feel I could have sorted myself out.

But I still wish it had been possible to speak to Barbara
again – even now I would like to know how it was for
her. I feel very responsible although nobody seemed to
want that.

It is clear from the interviews that men do have feelings
about abortion and it is also possible to see how easily their
behaviour and their uncertainty about what role to play can
be misunderstood. It also seems that men are more likely to
feel concerned about the welfare of the woman and the
impact of abortion on the relationship than to suffer over
the issue of morality, of life and death which so affects many
women.

Another point which needs making is that men who do
listen, who do attempt truly to empathize with what they
are going through, can make a huge difference to the way a
woman feels about her experience. Margery says:

Dave is not a great one for talking but when we found I
was pregnant he held me every night for the week we
talked about it, listened, told me that he would support
whatever choice I felt was best and I really felt that there
was no pressure to have or not to have an abortion. I
knew he would have been prepared to start a family and
care for it. In the end, that didn't seem a good decision
but I know his involvement, his feeling that it absolutely
was his problem too made me feel very protected and
able to cope.

There are probably far more men who behave this way than we hear about, for it tends to be the stories of treachery which are remembered. All the men interviewed have said that they wished there was someone they could have talked to about their situation – whether a friend or a counselling service. To offer men support and help in abortion is not in any way to undermine the importance of women being in charge of their own bodies, but it is to acknowledge that a pregnancy is the meeting of male and female and is a mutual responsibility. If the two people in a relationship want to remain together, there need to be ways for the man's responsibility and feelings to be recognized.

10. Abortion Information

Deciding that you must have an abortion may be the first step, but it is surprising how many people discover, having made this decision, that they do not know how to set about getting one.

Getting what you want, the best experience possible in the circumstances, may well rest on the information you have, on feeling you have made an informed choice, that you know where to go and what to expect. For all the supportive and helpful GPs and consultants around, there are some who take a hostile line on abortion, who will seek to make women feel bad about their choice and who may actively prevent them from having a termination. This will never be pleasant or easy to deal with but at least if you know that you are entitled to consult a different GP or to go to a private charity or clinic without referral from your doctor it can minimize the distress.

Equally, knowing what to expect when you go for the operation is important. Not everyone wants the full details of what the operation entails, although if you do you should insist on being told, but it may well be sensible to have some idea of what is involved, rather than wondering and suffering in ignorance afterwards. It is also wise to have some idea of what degree of pain or bleeding is 'normal' after the operation, and what to do if things do not seem right.

Morning-after (post-coital) birth control

If you know you have had unprotected intercourse – for example, if you have unexpectedly had sex, if a condom has broken, if you have forgotten to take the Pill – it is possible to interrupt conception by either of the two following methods:

1. A dose of hormones is given in the form of two tablets to be taken in the clinic and two to be taken 12 hours later. It is believed that the pills are most effective if taken within 48 hours of intercourse; 72 is the outside limit. The failure rate has been estimated at about 1 per cent.

2. In some circumstances doctors will fit an intrauterine device (a coil) which has a 100 per cent success rate. It can then be used as a form of contraception or can be removed at the next period.

This morning-after birth control is offered at BPAS and PAS, Brook and some family planning clinics. It is regarded as emergency treatment – not a method of regular birth control.

Finding out whether you are pregnant

If you think you may be pregnant, find out as quickly as possible. A missed period is the most obvious indication but even without this nausea, vomiting and retching, sore breasts, lethargy, needing to pass water frequently, can be symptoms of pregnancy.

If someone does not want to be pregnant, it is quite understandable that she may avoid finding out for sure and having to face the problem. But it is essential to do so, as the pregnancy gets considerably harder to cope with if you terminate late rather than early.

Pregnancy tests can be done by your doctor, but GPs frequently send samples away to be tested, which can take as long as two weeks. Most chemists sell home pregnancy testing kits. Many cannot be used until two weeks after a missed period, but there is now a new variety which can be used the first day after a period is missed.

Home pregnancy tests are fairly reliable but they do have a failure rate so if you get a negative result but go on missing

a period and/or having pregnancy symptoms, it is important to get another test done by a doctor or clinic within two
weeks. And if you miss a second period it is most important
to get a test done as soon as possible.

The charities BPAS and PAS will do pregnancy tests,
although you will have to pay, but some family planning
clinics offer a free test if you prefer this to consulting your
GP. Brook will do it free but they do ask for a donation
towards costs. The charities all do tests on the spot so you
get instant results.

Seeking help in making the decision

It is most important to find a friend or professional to discuss the situation with. A great many women, however
regretfully it may be, decide they must choose termination
and for them the opportunity to talk through the issues will
be a useful form of therapy, a way of reassuring themselves
that this really is what must be done. For other women,
talking through their feelings, ambivalences, fears, uncer-
tainties is a necessary process by which they can examine
different options and decide that they do or do not want
termination.

A GP should provide neutral counselling, asking the
woman how she feels about the situation, allowing her the
chance to explore the implications of having or not having a
baby if she wishes, supporting her in whichever decision
she makes. If yours does not, try to cling to the fact that it is
not a doctor's role to pontificate on a woman's morals. He
or she is there, paid by the taxpayer, to serve the patient as
client. If he or she is unprepared to do this you are entitled
to go to another doctor in the same practice or outside to
seek more constructive help.

If you do not wish to discuss the situation with your doctor but feel counselling would be helpful in making the initial decision, BPAS and PAS offer this service for a small

fee, while Brook do it free but ask for a donation towards costs.

The aim of counselling at the charities is to allow you to express all your feelings about the situation. The counsellors do not have any interest in persuading women to have abortions. Their interest is in questioning and talking to women in a way which will draw from them honest and sometimes unacknowledged feelings about what they want to do. As Caroline Bailey at Brook says, 'We certainly have women who, after talking, decide they will go ahead and have the baby. But we find that most girls and women when they come to us have made the decision and want the chance to look at how they feel and are likely to feel; to hear somebody talking who does not judge them bad.'

The legal situation

Although abortion was legalized when David Steel's Medical Termination Bill became law as the Abortion Act in 1967, the dispute over who should be allowed terminations and under what circumstances has continued. The law states that termination may be carried out provided that two registered medical practitioners agree that:
1. Your life is at greater risk by continuing the pregnancy than by terminating it.
2. Your physical or mental health is more likely to be injured by continuing with the pregnancy than by terminating it.
3. The physical or mental health of any existing children you have is more likely to be injured by your continuing with the pregnancy than by terminating it.
4. There is a reasonable chance the baby may be abnormal or deformed.

In making the decision doctors may take into account the woman's actual or reasonably foreseeable environment. Married women do not require a husband's consent for abortion, but a girl under 16 years must have the consent of one parent. This ruling applies throughout England and Wales, but in Northern Ireland and the Republic of Ireland abortion is illegal unless the continuance of pregnancy is thought to endanger the mother's life. In Scotland the Act applies as in England, but women must have the consent of a hospital consultant before a GP can refer for termination.

The Abortion Act contains a conscience clause which states that those with a conscientious objection to abortion are not obliged to participate in or perform abortion. For this and other reasons, your GP may refuse to support your termination.

So what do you do if a GP says he will not refer you to a consultant or sign the necessary green form? You can either try to see another doctor in the practice (if it is a group practice) or you can find another local GP to consult on this occasion. Otherwise, you can ring around local hospitals to see if they will give you an appointment to see a consultant. Clearly, if you are planning to do this it is worth trying to discover whether the hospital has a consultant sympathetic to abortion.

It may be that your GP is sympathetic but refers you to a consultant who decides that you do not have a case for termination. In this case you will have to return to your GP and hope he or she can refer you to a different consultant who will agree to what you want – of course all this will delay the process. Not surprisingly a good many women decide at this point to go private if they can.

There is no fixed period of time between seeing a GP and getting an appointment with a consultant. It can be just a few days, it can be three weeks. Then there will be another wait – usually about a week to ten days – between getting the consultant's agreement and having the operation performed.

There is plenty of evidence to show that women who are refused help by a doctor may end up having a 'late' abortion

– that is abortion after 14 weeks which is more unpleasant than early abortion and carries a greater risk. For this reason it is essential to seek help as soon as you have made up your mind you want a termination, or feel uncertain and want counselling.

Once two doctors have agreed that you can have an abortion, a date should be set for the operation. The length of time you will have to wait varies from one health area to another. If you can get referred to one of the NHS day-care clinics, there should not be a long wait.

For those who can afford them, there is always the option of the private abortion.

Private abortions

The private abortion service is set up to function quickly and efficiently. If the situation is straightforward women can expect to get an appointment for the operation within five to ten days of seeing the counsellor and the doctors.

Private abortions are offered by charities which operate on a non-profit-making basis, or by private clinics which are profit-making. The cost may not differ much, but it has been suggested that some private clinics are not all that concerned with women's welfare and it is worth going to one of the well-known, registered charities if you can. The best known are the British Pregnancy Advisory Service (BPAS) and the Pregnancy Advisory Service (PAS). Addresses on p. 136 following.

Methods of abortion

If your abortion is done within 12 weeks it will involve a very simple procedure which, basically, involves stretching the neck of the womb and clearing out the contents. This is done through the vagina and may be done under local anaesthetic if you go to a day-care clinic, but many women prefer to have a general anaesthetic. It is known as an 'early' abortion.

The best time for the operation is around nine weeks. Earlier than this there is a chance that the tiny foetus may be missed and left in the uterus.

NHS practitioners often insist that they will not perform these 'early' abortions after three months, but some doctors in the private sector are prepared to do vaginal terminations up until 14 weeks, if they judge it safe. After four months, or where the 'early' kind of abortion is not suitable, a different method, induction, is used.

Induction takes considerably longer than the 'early' kind of abortion and means that the woman must go into labour and 'deliver' the foetus. This is done by an injection into the womb of substances which are produced naturally by the body in a full-term labour, and which cause the womb to contract – in the way it would if you had a spontaneous miscarriage. The procedure generally takes about 12 hours but may last longer. It is usually necessary to spend two or possibly three nights in the hospital or clinic.

Side effects

Some women bleed fairly heavily after an 'early' termination so it is not a good idea to be too energetic during the 48 hours following. If you are bleeding heavily, it may be necessary to go to bed. It is important to make sure you do have time to rest afterwards. Any operation puts stress on the body and there is always a risk of complications if you get too exhausted.

The bleeding after abortion varies. Some women will bleed, although not too heavily, for days and even weeks. For others it may be just a couple of days. If the bleeding does go on, heavily, for more than two or three days contact your doctor or the organization which handled your operation and check that all is well.

You may get cramps after the operation, and you may pass blood like-clots. Again the degree of pain is different for different women and it is worth taking a few pain killers for the first couple of days afterwards. But as with the bleeding, if the pain continues seek help. Any sharp or unexpected pain or a rise in temperature or other symptoms of illness should be reported to a doctor immediately.

Women having late abortions do sometimes find that their breasts produce milk for a few days after and the breasts may be painful.

As the neck of the womb cannot be sterilized before the operation and as it remains slightly open for a while after the operation, there is a very slight risk of infection. To minimize this risk avoid using tampons or other internal protection. Do not sit or lie in a bath for a week after the operation. Penetrative sex should be avoided for at least two weeks.

Following the abortion

The interviews done for this book indicate a very real need for some kind of post-abortion counselling or help to be available for women and men. It is clear that many people feel distressed by their experience and would like the opportunity to talk about it, to share their feelings with others in a similar situation. The Women's Therapy Centre in London does run post-abortion groups. BPAS, PAS and Brook all give post-abortion counselling to women who want it. If you are very distressed and upset afterwards it is sensible to see your doctor and ask about referral to a therapist. Women who get trapped with their feelings of guilt and distress do sometimes get severely depressed and this can be avoided with therapeutic help.

Organizations

Brook Advisory Centres
Central Office
153a East Street
London SE17
Tel: 01-708-1234

Scottish Office
50 Lower Gilmore Place
Edinburgh
Scotland SE17 25D
Tel: 031-229-3596

Brook offers a service primarily for young women. Besides pregnancy counselling and referral, this includes birth control advice, supplies and pregnancy tests. A pregnancy test costs £2 but otherwise their service is free, although they do ask for donations.

Opening times include evenings and Saturday mornings. There are centres in Birmingham (4 centres), Bristol, Coventry, Liverpool, London (11 centres) and Edinburgh. They try to refer for abortions on the NHS and 75% get them. They will make appointments and set up the operation for women. Otherwise they refer to PAS.

British Pregnancy Advisory Service (BPAS)
Head Office is at:
Austy Manor
Wootton Wowen
Solihull
West Midlands
Tel: Henley-in-Arden 3225

BPAS was formed 17 years ago and is now a national, registered charity. It provides pregnancy tests, information, counselling and abortions as well as advice on contraception, infertility and sexuality. For a small fee, pregnancy tests are available at all branches. The cost for an abortion is as low as they are able to make it – in 1985 it was around £150. They have nursing homes throughout the country.

Pregnancy Advisory Service (PAS)
11–13 Charlotte Street
London W1
Tel: 01-637-8962

PAS offers pregnancy counselling and abortion and other services which include cervical smears, post-coital contraception, female sterilization. They have one clinic in Greater London.

Ulster Pregnancy Advisory Service
338a Lisburn Road
Belfast
N. Ireland
Tel: Belfast 667345

As abortion is illegal in Ireland the Ulster Pregnancy Advisory Service do not perform operations, but they do offer counselling.

LIFE
118–120 Warwick Street
Leamington Spa
Warwickshire
Tel: 0926-21587

LIFE is a charity which offers counselling to pregnant women. They also offer housing for up to 12 months to women who are feeling forced into abortion because they have nowhere to live and are short of money. However,

LIFE is opposed to abortion and their approach will therefore be to encourage continuing the pregnancy.

Society for the Protection of the Unborn Child (SPUC)
7 Tufton Street
London SW1
Tel: 01-222-5845

SPUC is a campaigning and pressure group which aims to have the Abortion Act repealed because it disapproves of abortion.

Family Planning Information Service (FPA)
27-35 Mortimer Street
London W1
Tel: 01-636-7866

4 Clifton Street
Glasgow
Tel: 041-333-9696

The FPA provides advice and leaflets on family planning, and the addresses of clinics. They will organize some pregnancy tests.

Women's Reproductive Rights Information Centre
52–54 Featherstone Street
London EC1
Tel: 01-251-6332

This organization combines campaigning for improvements in the abortion service with offering an information service to individual women, women's groups, schools, etc. They also offer support to women who do not know where to find the help they need and women who have suffered abuses within the health system and want to talk about it.

They produce a list of health pamphlets available from their office.

The Birth Control Campaign (BCC)
27–35 Mortimer Street
London W1
Tel: 01-580-9360

This pressure group campaigns for better National Health Service abortion, contraception and sterilization services.

The Birth Control Trust (BCT)
Address as BCC.

The BCT is a charity which co-ordinates information on abortion and other areas of family planning; they campaign for improvements in services; they have an information service for people studying the above subjects. They publish a range of pamphlets and books including several on aspects of abortion.

The Abortion Law Reform Association (ALRA)
88a Islington High Street
London N1
Tel: 01-359-5200

ALRA was established in 1963 by a group of people concerned at the scale and consequences of back-street abortion. They contributed to getting the 1967 Abortion Act passed. They continue to campaign for improvements in the Act. Their campaign, run under the slogan 'A Woman's Right to Choose', is also concerned with defending the Act from attempts by anti-abortionists to make it harder to get abortions or to have legal abortion banned altogether.

The National Abortion Campaign (NAC)

374 Gray's Inn Road
London WC1
Tel: 01-278-0153

NAC has been going for ten years and is one of the best-known campaigning organizations working from the absolute conviction that abortion must be a woman's decision. They carry out surveys of facilities around the country, and aim to get improved facilities and support for women when they need an NHS abortion.

The Women's Therapy Centre
6 Manor Gardens
London N7
Tel: 01-263-6200

The Centre offers workshops on issues affecting women, including post-abortion support, depression, massage and relaxation.

Abortion Anonymous Counselling Service
Tel: 01-350-2229

This is a phone-in help line for women who have had abortions and want to speak to someone. The counsellors are trained volunteers. Although it is primarily aimed at women wanting post-abortion support, advice will be given to pregnant women wanting help and to people wanting contraceptive advice.

Well Woman Clinic
Eccles Street
Dublin
Tel: 000-1-381-365

Although abortion is illegal in the Republic of Ireland, this clinic provides a pregnancy and abortion counselling service. If you decide that you want an abortion, the clinic will arrange for you to be booked into a hospital in England and for you to see a GP in England. The clinic does pregnancy tests.

Summing Up

Abortion is not a happy choice, as the women (and men) speaking here make plain.

Women who most profoundly do not want to have abortions go ahead and do so not because they are pressurized into it by what SPUC describes as our 'abortion culture' or because abortion is so easily available that women use it as contraception, as some suggest, but because they cannot see an alternative. And the pain in making this choice is, for many women, that it goes against fundamental beliefs and values they hold: abortion is an issue where moral absolutes do not and cannot exist for a great many people.

Those who oppose abortion and would see the Act repealed seem to believe that the pain and distress women experience over abortion would disappear if only they could be prevented from being able to get abortions and thus to have to face the decision to terminate life. But this is manifestly not true.

Research demonstrates that unwanted children may be at best resented, at worst maltreated. Making abortion illegal is not an answer. History shows that when legal abortion is not available women get illegal ones with even worse psychological and physical effects to both foetus and mother.

There is no straightforward answer to the pain women experience over abortion, because the meaning of the experience, the circumstances, the relationship surrounding it, are different in every case. And each woman is different: some cope fairly easily with abortion, others go through prolonged distress. However, the conditions under which women get their abortions, the way they are treated by medical practitioners, the amount of support they receive make an enormous difference to the way they will ultimately feel.

The woman who feels that she has made her own decision about abortion with support from partner and/or friends, who is backed up in making her own decision by GP and consultant and who can have the abortion as quickly as possible, will feel less distress than a woman who is condemned for choosing abortion, or who is coerced into it, who has no-one with whom to talk the situation through and who meets hostility and disapproval from medical practitioners.

An awful lot of women are made to suffer when they go for abortions and who can doubt that the woman who is made to feel cheap and dirty by her doctor, who is humiliated by her consultant, feels a guilty secrecy about what has happened? It is not difficult to imagine that, having decided an abortion is what must be done, a woman feels considerably worse when faced with a four- or five-week delay.

And this is where the pro-choice lobby is right in pressing on for improvements in the abortion service. A law exists which permits abortion but it is a law which leaves the granting of it primarily in the hands of men – who will never have to experience the dilemma of abortion and who may well have personal reasons for disliking it.

It is doctors and those policy-makers they advise who are all too often responsible for the quality of the abortion experience, for the degree of suffering a woman may endure. They are wilfully making the abortion experience worse than it needs to be.

It is important that women feel they can and should talk about their feelings about abortion. While most intimate areas of life have been opened up for discussion in recent years, abortion still carries a veil of secrecy; people who have chosen termination continue to feel flawed and judged. Those women who have talked about their experiences, who have found that far from being alone they are one of the many experiencing mixed feelings, are comforted and helped by the process.

Notes

1. Linda Gordon, *Woman's Body, Woman's Rights*, Penguin, 1977.
2. Marion Hall and Raymond Illsley, 'Psychological Aspects of Abortion', *Bulletin of the World Health Organization*, Vol. 53, 1976.
3. Kristin Lukas, *The Politics of Motherhood*, University of California Press, 1984.
4. Sara Maitland, 'Catholicism in Conflict', Jubilee Lecture published by the Jubilee Group, 1982.
5. Kathleen McDonnell, *Not An Easy Choice*, The Women's Press, Ontario, 1984.
6. Judith Bury, *Teenage Pregnancy in Britain*, The Birth Control Trust, 1984.
7. Isabel Allen, *Family Planning, Sterilization and Abortion Services*, Policy Studies Institute, 1985.
8. Linda Clarke, *Camden Abortion Survey*, British Pregnancy Advisory Service, 1983.
9. John Ashton, Journal of Biosocial Science, Vol. 12, 1980.
10. Sara Maitland, *In Vitro Veritas*, St Mary's, Bourne Street, London, 1984.
11. Kathleen McDonnell, *op. cit.*
12. Germaine Greer, *Sex and Destiny*, Picador, 1984.
13. Gillian Clarke, *Woman's Views: An Investigation into Consumer Evaluation of Abortion Services*, Department of Psychology, Surrey University, 1985.
14. Isabel Allen, *Counselling Services for Sterilization, Vasectomy and Termination of Pregnancy*, Policy Studies Institute, 1985.
15. Isabel Allen, *ibid*.

16. Madelaine Simms, *Report on Non-Medical Abortion Counselling*, Birth Control Trust, 1973, revised 1977.
17. Lane Committee Report, 1974.
18. Isabel Allen, *Counselling Services for Sterilization, Vasectomy and Termination of Pregnancy*, Policy Studies Institute, 1985.
19. Linda Clarke, *op. cit.*
20. Royal College of Obstetricians and Gynaecologists, *Late Abortions in England and Wales*, 1984.
21. Isabel Allen, *Family Planning, Sterilization and Abortion Services*, Policy Studies Institute, 1985.
22. Royal College of Obstetricians and Gynaecologists, *op. cit.*
23. Linda Clarke, *op. cit.*
24. John Ashton, *op. cit.*
25. Isabel Allen, *Counselling Services for Sterilization, Vasectomy and Termination of Pregnancy*, Policy Studies Institute, 1985.
26. Julia South, *New Statesman*, 22 November 1985.
27. Royal College of Obstetricians and Gynaecologists, *op. cit.*
28. Marion Hall and Raymond Illsely, *op. cit.*
29. Germaine Greer, *op. cit.*
30. R.F. Gardner, *Abortion – The Personal Dilemma*, Paternoster Press, 1972.
31. Annabel Broome, *Nursing Mirror*, 16 May 1984.
32. John Ashton, 'The Psychosocial Outcome of Induced Abortion', *British Journal of Obstetrics and Gynaecology*, Vol. 87, December 1980.
33. M. Clark *et al*, 'Sequels of Unwanted Pregnancy', *Lancet*, 31 August 1968.
34. Marion Hall and Raymond Illsley, *op. cit.*
35. C.M.B. Pare and H. Raven, 'Follow-Up of Patients Referred for Termination of Pregnancy', *Lancet*, 28 March 1970.

36. John Robinson, *Christian Freedom in a Permissive Society*, S.C.M. Press, 1970. (Reprint of a lecture to the Abortion Law Reform Association, 1966.)
37. Edward Patey, quoted by Sara Maitland, *op. cit.*

OTHER BOOKS FROM PLUTO

THE HEARTS OF MEN
American Dreams and the Flight from Commitment
BARBARA EHRENREICH

Writing with conviction and wit, Barbara
Ehrenreich traces men's rejection of the
breadwinner ethic. She contends that it was this
defiance of 'responsibility' which fuelled the
right-wing, anti-feminist movement.

'Compelling analysis'. *Guardian*
'Written in a lively journalistic style, with a
cool undertow of humour… a gentle polemic…
The Hearts of Men is an admirable piece of
feminist strategy.' *City Limits*
'A good read, and gives an element of hope
to feminists with men in their lives.' *Tribune*

224 pages
0 86104 724 9   £4.95 paperback

ONLY THE RIVERS RUN FREE
Northern Ireland – the Women's War
EILEEN FAIRWEATHER, ROISIN McDONOUGH and MELANIE McFADYEAN

This book is a moving account of the lives of women in the Catholic and Protestant ghettos of war-torn Northern Ireland. The authors have recorded interviews with women who are oppressed by male violence, sexual ignorance, repressive churches, and the racist and prejudiced 'security' forces; with women who are involved in politics; and women who are working to alleviate the misery of poverty.

Only the Rivers Run Free is a mixture of the words of Irish women and descriptions of their circumstances, but not all of it is grim. There is the humour of a highly articulate working class and their hopes for the future.

Among the women interviewed are volunteers with the IRA, Mrs Paisley, prisoners in Armagh, as well as many others not directly involved in the conflict. *Only the Rivers Run Free* is a unique account of the tribulations of ordinary women in a society at war.

'A powerful, heart-rending piece of journalism.' *Guardian*

'The truth of how women cope in Northern Ireland in their marriages, their religion, their poverty and in war.' Dolours Price, *Fortnight*

352 pages
0 86104 668 4   **£5.95 paperback**

GENDER AT WORK
ANN GAME and ROSEMARY PRINGLE
Introduction by Cynthia Cockburn

The number of trades and professions in which
women work is increasing. Newspapers dearly
love 'the first woman taxi-driver' stories. They
neglect areas, including housework, where
women's presence is a long-established reality.
The case studies in *Gender at Work* – on
manufacturing, banking, the retail trade,
computers, nursing and housework – reflect
established trends occurring in all advanced
capitalists countries, including the UK. Its
empirical richness makes the book essential
reading for everyone interested in
understanding the link between the oppression
of women through production in workplaces
and consumption at home.

    'A welcome addition to the literature.'
Tribune
    'One of the most interesting contributions to
women's studies to be published in a long
while.' Ursula Huws, *City Limits*

144 pages
0 86104 671 4   £3.95 paperback

Pluto books are available through your local
bookshop. In case of difficulty contact Pluto to
find out local stockists or to obtain catalogues/
leaflets (telephone 01-482 1973).
    If all else fails write to:

Pluto Press Limited
Freepost (no stamp required)
105A Torriano Avenue
London NW5 1YP